You Get To
Make It Up

A SMART Living 365 Guide to

Creating a Happy & Meaningful Life

Kathy Gottberg

You Get To Make It Up

A SMART Living 365 Guide to
Creating a Happy & Meaningful Life

Cover Design and Illustration: Thom Gottberg

ISBN: 9781699871393

ACKNOWLEDGMENTS

Everything I've ever done or written was done with the help and support of others. Everyone in my life has touched and helped me in one way or another. However, I specifically share incredible gratitude for my husband Thom who is my biggest fan and muse.

I owe a debt of gratitude to three "Accountability Partners" who helped me with reading this book and offering feedback. They are Julie Moore, Beverly Ducatte, and Pam Paradis. Your generosity of time and talent is highly valued and appreciated. I also owe gratitude to Gary Lange, Lessley Currier, Kay Wolff and Liesbet Collaert for their valuable final proofing. I hope you know how important you are!

In addition, I want to thank the hundreds of followers on my blog SMART Living 365.com. It is because of you that I know what information should be included in this book. You told me what you liked and what you found helpful and it is my sincere hope that these words reach out and touch those who can benefit most from this important change to your mind, heart and lifestyle.

Finally, I want to be sure to acknowledge and thank all of you who have read any of my books and then recommended them to others. With thousands of other authors in the world, and millions of blogs and books to choose from, the absolute best way to get exposure for my work is from you—the readers. So if you find any of my writing helpful, especially this book, I would be forever grateful if you would take the time to write a review of it on Amazon.com. If you have done so in the past, "Thank you!" and if you plan to in the future, "Thank you again!" My connection with you is a sweet and significant part of what I create.

TABLE OF CONTENTS

Introduction

We become what we think about all day long." ~Ralph Waldo Emerson

Are you happy? Do you wake up most days with eagerness and optimism for the day ahead or do you groan and roll over and hope for more sleep? I realize we all define happiness in different ways so I'm not limiting this discussion to that giddy sense of wellbeing that so many people think of as "happy". Instead, what I consider to be happiness is peace of mind, contentment, feeling relevant and necessary in your world, along with the deep joy of gratitude that makes life feel worthwhile. Happiness obviously can and will look very different to us all. Still, I believe it is possible to boil it down to the question: Are you happy? Because if your answer is no, then why not? Perhaps that's because you've forgotten, or didn't realize, that you really can "make it up."

I've been interested in this topic and related questions most of my life. However, I do realize that this idea can be challenging to some, especially if you've faced hardship throughout your life. But after studying hundreds of those who have faced tremendously difficult odds, I have discovered that it is possible, even then, "to make it up." I am convinced that while we may not be able to change the exact circumstances that happen in our lives, we can always change how we respond and where we go next. I'm not claiming it is easy or uncomplicated, but I am claiming it is possible. How do I know this is true? Because my life proves it over and over again.

But don't just take my word for it. In the following pages I share different thoughts that I've written about it on my blog SMART Living 365 during the last eight years. While I've done my best to share research and the work of scientists, psychologists, philosophers and other thought teachers when possible, it usually pares down to whether you are open to the idea in the first place. Similar to the Zen-saying about enlightenment—if you are receptive to the experience, then a leaf can fall on you and you are transformed. If not, a tree can fall on you and it will make no difference. Again, you get to make it up.

Unfortunately, most of us weren't raised to believe we can design our lives the way we want. In fact, I've read stories about how many people spend more time planning their wedding or their vacation than they do planning their lives. Then a few years or a few decades into it, some find themselves feeling like a hamster on a wheel. They are running as fast as they can but not getting anywhere. Even if that running looks successful on the outside, it can be like the Lily Tomlin quote that says, "The problem with winning the rat race is that you are still a rat."

It doesn't have to be that way. We do have choices. We can make it up. I'm not talking about how a magician tricks us into believing something that isn't true. I'm talking more like an alchemist that takes what is happening and converts it into something that brings us to a place where we are able to keep going and believing life is worth living. As said by Paulo Coelho in his book, *The Alchemist*, "…when you really want something to happen, the whole universe will conspire so that your wish comes true." An alchemist designs the course of his life and the universe helps it unfold.

I realize that these ideas sound almost too simple to be true. But again, much of a person's willingness to hear them will depend upon what they have been taught and conditioned to believe in their past. Still, if you aren't happy or fulfilled, or you just suspect that life is more than what you've been living, why not give it a chance? While this book is much too short and the concept much too complex to cover thoroughly between these pages, it is my intention that some of the chapters will at least intrigue you enough to continue.

That's actually what happened to my husband Thom and I nearly 35 years ago. We were both feeling stuck and uncertain about the treadmill of our lives and weren't quite sure where to go next. It was at that time we found ourselves in a bookstore and Thom picked up a very small book with probably only 150 pages titled, ***SuperBeings—The Superselling Guide To Finding Your Higher Self*** by John Randolph Price. What an odd title! Personally, I would never have picked it up with a title like that. But something about the book resonated with Thom. He bought it, we read it, and that began a journey of designing a life that has been more joyful, rewarding and purposeful than we ever imagined. Of course our lives haven't been struggle or pain free. But we now know we can always rely on some of the ideas that were planted so many years ago in order to turn our future around and move onward.

While I certainly can't "make it up" for anyone else other than myself, it is my sincere desire that the following pages either introduce you or encourage you to follow the path of designing a happy and fulfilling life for yourself. Just never forget that you can choose to be happy, healthy and live life to its fullest. Remember, you get to make it up!

Chapter One

The Science Behind "You Get To Make It Up!"

> *"I was exhilarated by the new
> realization that I could change the
> character of my life by changing my
> beliefs. I was instantly energized because
> I realized that there was a science-based
> path that would take me from my job as
> a perennial 'victim' to my new position
> as 'co-creator' of my destiny."*
> ~ *Dr. Bruce H. Lipton*

Around 25 years ago Thom came up with the phrase, "you get to make it up." Something about that statement rang true with many of the people we knew. But at the same time the phrase raised questions, like: What the...? You mean I am making it up when bad things happen and I don't feel good? I get to make up who is the next president? I am making it up when I'm broke and in debt? It sounds so bold, presumptive and sacrilegious to say we are individually making it all up. But after reading a new book entitled, Subliminal—***How Your***

Unconscious Mind Rules Your Behavior there is now neuroscientific proof that much of what happens in our lives is indeed the creation of our own minds.

Of course I should begin by agreeing that if you stand in the road in front of a speeding car you will be severely hurt. No matter how much you want to believe that you are invisible, and that a car can pass right through you, it isn't going to happen. If you jump out of an airplane without a parachute, you will smash when you hit the ground. The laws of nature are stronger than your mind so let go of that argument right from the beginning. But what you do have control over is whether you jump out of that airplane without a parachute, or whether you mindlessly walk into the middle of a busy street. You also determine what happens to you once you are hurt—and you are equally the creator of the story you will tell about it should you survive.

So what do you make up? Dr. Leonard Mlodinow explains this concept in his book, *Subliminal—How Your Unconscious Mind Rules Your Behavior.* He is also the author of several other books and a theoretical physicist that teaches at the California Institute of Technology. The big idea behind the book is that the latest scientific research proves that our unconscious mind largely shapes the experiences of our world. Mlodinow says, "Your preferences in politicians, the amount you tip your waiter—all judgments and perceptions reflect the workings of our mind on two levels: the conscious, of which we are aware, and the unconscious, which is hidden from us." And while most of us want to believe that we are aware, awake and consciously making choices each minute, much of the time we are just going through the motions.

Mlodinow continues, "The point is that we are not like computers that crunch data in a relatively straightforward manner and calculate results. Instead, our brains are made up of a collection of many modules that work in parallel, with complex interactions, most of which operate outside our consciousness. As a consequence, the real reasons behind our judgments, feelings, and behaviors can surprise us."

What are some of the surprises? First, there is plenty of research about food choices that prove our unconscious choices on a regular basis. According to research, people "decide" how much to eat based upon the box size as much as taste. In addition, when the size of a container of snack food is doubled, food consumption automatically INCREASES 30 to 45 percent of the time. We routinely make purchases based upon the colors and shapes of the containers and there are also studies that show that when a food item is described in a fancy and elaborate way, people rate the food as literally TASTING better.

Or what about how much you will pay for your food? Experiments show that people are willing to pay 40 to 61percent more for an item of junk food if they see it sitting right in front of them versus seeing it behind Plexiglas or in a photo in a magazine. There is also plenty of evidence that normal wine drinkers cannot judge much difference between cost and taste. But, if people drink a wine that is more expensive it actually TASTES better to those being polled. In fact, when subjects had their brains scanned by an fMRI while drinking wine they judged as very expensive and flavorful, the area in the brain behind the eyes associated with pleasure was highly activated. Mlodinow claims, "…when you run cool wine over your tongue, you don't just taste its chemical composition; you taste its price." He continues with, "Our brains are not simply recording a taste or other experience, they are CREATING it."

In other words, when we eat or enjoy something that we think has value, our unconscious mind is actually "making up" that value based upon what fits into our current beliefs. That's why some people can get really excited about a certain handbag by a famous designer and another person, like me, has zero interest. What we routinely forget is that we are choosing, or else feeding, our belief systems on a regular basis—and then we "make up" and live out of our unconscious reactions to those beliefs most of the time.

Mlodinow goes on in his book to explain even more experiments that prove that our unconscious minds help to create the world we are experiencing. Just about all of us routinely buy products and services that we are already familiar with without considering there might be something much better available. We purchase stocks when the names are easy to pronounce, tip waiters more when the sun is shining, and vote for political candidates purely on looks alone 69 to 72 percent of the time. We mistakenly imprison people with inaccurate eyewitness identification up to 75 percent of the time (!!!!) and incorrectly remember life events anywhere from 26 to 80% of the time. According to Mlodinow, when we remember things that happened in the past, most of us "smooth out memories" so that they make sense to us. One of the studies quoted says, "Whenever anything appeared incomprehensible, it was either omitted or explained by adding content." All of that editing and adding is based upon what we already believe to be true. Again, what we see, hear, choose and remember is largely dependent upon what already fits inside our minds—in other words, we are "making it up!"

I think most of us know that many of the activities of our bodies and our minds are unconscious. While I'm sitting here my heart is beating, my hormones are doing their thing and my breakfast is being digested along with thousands of other automatic responses. Unfortunately, what most of us are less aware of is that some scientists estimate that we are fully conscious only 5% of the time—the remaining 95% of the time we are basically asleep (unconscious). Mlodinow says, "We believe that when we choose a laptop or a laundry detergent, plan a vacation, pick a stock, take a job, assess a sports star, make a friend, judge a stranger and even fall in love, we understand the principal factors that influenced us. Very often nothing could be further from the truth. As a result, many of our most basic assumptions about ourselves and society are false."

So what does this information mean for you and me? Most importantly it is a reminder that the world we live in and experience is constantly being judged, motivated and influenced by our existing belief system. That belief system is a collection of the memories, input and stimulation we have absorbed in our past. Then when confronted with any experience or circumstance in the present, our unconscious will automatically search our belief system for easy and automatic responses and fill it in when necessary to round out the experience. If our belief system is primarily negative—the experience will automatically be filled in with negative responses. If our belief system sways to the positive—no matter what happens, then the circumstance will be created with a positive spin. We are making it up! Our responses, our judgments, our reactions, our choices, are largely dependent upon what is already programmed into our present belief system.

The good news is that if we don't like our experience then it's time to get to work on what lies at the core of our beliefs about how we view the world. Who knows how those perceptions got there? Certainly, our upbringing, our culture and the focus of our attention serves to fill up the reservoir. While it is important to stay awake and conscious in our lives as much as possible, this information suggests that we would also be SMART to work on filling our unconscious with automatic responses that create a world to our liking. Don't like every aspect of your life? Then start today remembering that YOU get to make it up!

Chapter Two

What Did You Make Up Your Mind About Today?

"Each morning when I open my eyes I say to
myself: I, not events, have the power to make
me happy or unhappy today. I can choose
which it shall be. Yesterday is dead,
tomorrow hasn't arrived yet. I have just one
day, today, and I'm going to be happy in it."
~ Groucho Marx

My husband Thom had a rather cantankerous relationship with his mother. Bert, short for Roberta, had a very strong need for approval, especially from others. That led her to working every day to make Thom the perfect child. Unfortunately, the more she tried, the more rebellious he became. But even then, something she did do for him was to plant an extremely powerful seed in his mind. Ironically, rather than tell him directly, he overheard her saying it to a neighbor. That seed, that statement was, "Thom can do anything he sets his mind to." Not only did that seed sprout and take root, it's been a guiding principal in his life. And I'd bet, when you think about it, most of us live our entire lives based upon what we've set our mind to be, do, or have. Regrettably, many of us ignore the power of that set point as well as our ability to adjust it in a positive way by design.

Because I write so much about happiness and maintaining a positive attitude, I frequently hear others imply that it is easy for me because I have such a great life. But from my perspective, a big reason why I have such a great life is exactly because that is what "I've made up my mind" to have. While that might sound like bragging or even being delusional, I am actually just following in the footsteps of Abraham Lincoln. Some believe that Lincoln said, "Folks are usually about as happy as they make up their mind to be."

And Lincoln should know. In case you've forgotten, Lincoln had a very tumultuous life. History shows that Lincoln battled with sadness and depression his entire life. Not only did he fail in two business ventures, he lost a number of elections for public office, including the Vice-Presidency. His mother and sister died when he was young and his first fiancée died before they were married. Following that he had a nervous breakdown and was bed-ridden for six months. When he eventually did marry, he and his wife had four children with only one of them living to maturity. Yet in spite of all that loss and challenge he was able to say that we can be as happy as we make up our mind to be.

Of course, Lincoln wasn't the only person who said something along these lines. Here are a few other quotes from others that show the power of making up our minds to be happy.

"Make up your mind to be happy. Learn to find pleasure in simple things." ~Robert Louis Stevenson

"You can conquer almost any fear if you will only make up your mind to do so. Remember, fear doesn't exist anywhere except in the mind." ~Dale Carnegie

"It is your choice to be happy. Make up your mind to enjoy this day, to have a blessed, prosperous, victorious year. You may have some setbacks and your circumstances may change but don't let that change your mind. Keep it set to happiness." ~Joel Osteen

"It's been my experience that you can nearly always enjoy things if you make up your mind firmly that you will." ~Lucy Maud Montgomery

"If you want to be sad, no one in the world can make

you happy. But if you make up your mind to be happy, no one and nothing on earth can take that happiness from you." ~Paramhansa Yogananda

Okay, so suppose you agree with me and others that we all have the power to make up our mind to be happy. Why don't we do it? What keeps many of us from making this choice every single moment? I think the most obvious excuse comes from a guy named Robert Breault who said, "It's hard to make up your bed while you're still sleeping on it. Hard to make up your mind for the same reason."

Accepting that, here are five things that I think are necessary to help us make up our mind to be happy:

1) Stay Present And Mindful. Most of us are pretty sloppy with our thoughts. Like the blowing wind, we allow circumstances and distractions to take our thoughts in every direction nearly every moment of the day. As author and "Harvard Happiness Expert" Daniel Gilbert says in his book, ***Stumbling on Happiness:***

"People spend 46 percent of their waking hours thinking about something other than what they're doing, and this mind-wandering typically makes them unhappy... 'Mind-wandering is an excellent predictor of people's happiness,' Killingsworth says.

'In fact, how often our minds leave the present and where they tend to go is a better predictor of our happiness than the activities in which we are engaged.'… Time-lag analyses conducted by the researchers suggested that their subjects' mind-wandering was generally the cause, not the consequence, of their unhappiness."

2) Train Your Thoughts. It is very popular to get enough exercise and eat in a way that keeps a person healthy. But some people are far less discriminating about doing what it takes to train their mind and keep it healthy and happy. Sounds simple, right? But as author Anne Lamont says:

> *"Try looking at your mind as a wayward puppy that you are trying to paper train. You don't drop-kick a puppy into the neighbor's yard every time it piddles on the floor. You just keep bringing it back to the newspaper."*

3) Pay Attention To Your Self-Talk. Most of us would never, ever say certain things to people we care about. Yet, without even noticing, we often say some of the harshest and unkind things to ourselves over and over again. Anytime we put our negative emotions like fear and anger into words in our mind, we are feeding ourselves a toxic waste that destroys our happiness. Like sports star David James said:

"Be mindful of your self-talk. It's a conversation with the universe."

4) Hang Out With The Right People. I think we all intuitively know that the people who we spend the most time with have the power to influence both our health and our happiness. Research is going even further now by proving that that influence happens *even with the friends of the friends* we hang out with. If you want to make up your mind to be happier, then be very picky about the people you spend time with. As Mark Twain said:

"Keep away from people who try to belittle your ambitions. Small people always do that, but the really great make you feel that you too, can become great. When you are seeking to bring plans to fruition, it is important who you regularly associate. Hang out with friends who are like-minded and who are also designing purpose-filled lives. Similarly, be that kind of a friend for your friends."

5) Stay Focused And Determined To Be Happy. I realize that some of us have it easier than others to make up our mind about happiness. But instead of comparing our lives to those of us who have it easier, how about we take a look at all of those who have faced and triumphed over challenges much harder than ours and won. It is possible if we take the time, and if you're anything like me, I find that very inspiring. I'm like everyone else—I can complain or whine about some of the pain I've had in my life or I can make up my mind to create the life I want. As George Bernard Shaw said:

"People are always blaming their circumstances for what they are. I don't believe in circumstances. The people who get on in this world are the people who get up and look for the circumstances they want, and if they can't find them, make them."

Starting today, I am going to do my best to make up my mind to be happy no matter what. That doesn't mean I'm condoning bad actions or that I won't stay actively engaged at working to create a better world. But what it does mean is that in spite of any circumstances I am going to act as though happiness, hope and possibility are available to each and every one of us. Plus, as Earl Nightingale said, "We are all self-made, but only the successful will admit it." Just remember it's SMART to realize that every single one of us can set our mind to anything. Choose wisely.

Chapter Three

The Truth Behind "You Create Your Own Reality"

> *"The dream you are living is your creation.*
> *It is your perception of reality that you can*
> *change at any time. You have the power to*
> *create hell, and you have the power to create*
> *heaven. Why not dream a different*
> *dream?" ~Don Miguel Ruiz*

The phrase, "you create your own reality" has been part of the Western vernacular for at least several decades now. Originally a statement promoted by those with a more progressive perspective on life, the idea behind the phrase is now commonly found everywhere from books to television, to popular music and in movies. But while I'll admit that it is empowering to think I influence my world, and easy to imagine that your reality can be very different from mine, obviously that doesn't mean I can just flap my arms and fly just because I want to "create that." So what does the statement really mean? Is it true? And if yes, how does that lead to a

SMART and happy life?

First off, I think it is important to acknowledge that this is not just another new age statement. While the exact phrase, "you create your own reality" may have come from Jane Roberts back in the 1970's, others have expressed similar ideas for several millennia. The Buddha said, "What you dwell upon you become." Jesus said, "It is done unto you as you believe." Hindu mysticism from Shankaracharya says, "Whatever a person's mind dwells on intensely and with firm resolve, that is exactly what he becomes." It says in the Talmud, "We do not see things as they are, we see them as we are."

More recent sages like Ralph Waldo Emerson have said, "We become what we think about all day long." Walt Disney said, "If you can dream it you can do it." Napoleon Hill said, "Whatever the mind can conceive and believe it can achieve." Norman Vincent Peale said, "Change your thoughts and you change your world." Wayne Dyer says, "You see it when you believe it." And let's not forget Oprah who repeats this message frequently by saying things like, "Remember, you are co-creating your life with the energy of your own intentions."

Taking it even further is the work of Abraham-Hicks in their work *The Law Of Attraction.* I'll admit that I didn't start out as a fan of how LOA ideas were promoted through the movie **The Secret**. In my opinion, some of that movie seemed to reduce the entire point of existence on the planet to merely fulfilling our own personal desires and having all the "stuff" any person could ever want. However, after listening to more of Abraham-Hicks I have found underneath all that unconditional approval for how others create their own reality, there is actually a deeper message. That deeper message is one of empowerment where I am always THE CREATOR of my thoughts and actions. More importantly, that message points out that what most of us *really* want, even when we think we need "stuff" to make it happen, is to experience meaning, purpose, and well-being in our lives. Fortunately, with the proper focus that goal is within our ability.

Again, the message reminds me that regardless of the experience happening around me, how I respond, how I choose to perceive that experience is ALWAYS my choice. Even when the reality I am going through and observing is not perfect—in fact sometimes quite ugly—what I choose to take away from any of it is definitely my prerogative. And while I can't "fly" just because I think it would be fun, I can certainly purchase an airline ticket and go where I want, decide what to see and do on my "journey", and determine the people who accompany me day-in and day-out. From those perspectives, I do indeed create my own reality. Perhaps an even better way of thinking about it is that I create the EXPERIENCE of my reality each and every minute.

Another view on this idea came to me while listening to a talk by author and speaker Caroline Myss. A long-time fan, I've always appreciated Myss for her blunt honesty and insights. This topic was no exception. Myss does not deny that, "we create our own reality." Instead, she asks, "Why?" What does it matter if we create our own reality if all we are striving for is to get what we think we want in life? In her opinion, many of us are drawn to it for the sole purpose of creating a safer and more "controllable" life for ourselves. Instead, Myss suggests that the real meaning behind the idea of "we create our own reality" is because it is "meant to liberate us". She continues with, "It's meant to make you not like the life you have." Its primary purpose is to encourage a new idea of what our lives can be if we live courageously, honestly and full-out. She encourages us to ask ourselves, "How am I creating my reality? From what level?" Am I using it to access the bigger part of me or the smaller, fearful part that just wants to be safe?

Yet another perspective that offers an even wider view of the topic is the idea of co-creation or inter-being. On the surface, most of us tend to approach the idea of "creating our reality" from a surface level dualistic perspective. Maybe the best question is acknowledging a deep interconnection with the *Wholeness of Life Itself*. From that perspective, we are always constantly creating reality and having reality created around us, all at the same time at every moment. No duality. Only "One." That's why a word like co-creation acknowledges that we never act independently of *All-That-Is*, even when we like to think that we do.

What if creating our reality is less about making ourselves feel safe, protected and in control and more about trusting that we can be happy and at peace with the uncertainty of life no matter what occurs? Maybe it's less to do with making sure everything works perfectly in our favor, to instead seeing everything as it unfolds as already perfect. Chances are good we are alive and present at this time for much more than playing it safe and getting everything we ever thought we wanted. SMART Living 365 suggests that maybe, just maybe, conscious co-creating with the Universe is what we have been looking for all along.

Chapter Four

What Are You Nexting? The Power Of Positive Anticipation

"The best way to predict the future is to create it."
~Peter Drucker

One of the best words I came across this last year during my reading was the word "nexting." Used by author and research scientist Shane Lopez in his book **Making Hope Happen**, it describes the act of planning things in the future to look forward to, in a positive way. I've also been doing a lot of listening to Abraham-Hicks and the Law of Attraction where I've been continually reminded that what we think about and focus on is "attracted" automatically into our lives. In addition, as a long-time student of New Thought, I know that what I dwell upon largely becomes my day-to-day reality. So perhaps it would be wise for each of us to spend some time *nexting* the positive events we hope to experience during the coming months.

When you really think about it, taking the time to anticipate a positive future might be one of the highest priorities we can have. Like I've mentioned before, if we don't prioritize our lives, some *one* or some *thing* else will. Nexting helps us create our lives by design rather than default. Plus, by first recognizing the importance and then following through with the action of nexting, we are mind mapping what we would like to experience.

Where Did The Idea Of Nexting Begin?

Shane Lopez believes that nexting is a big part of making hope happen. As a research scientist dedicated to helping school systems come up with a better way to encourage students to learn, Lopez says nexting comes naturally to kids. He first came up with it when walking and talking with his son. Lopez says, "By encouraging (my son) to talk about the future, I find out what he is excited about. I learn about his plots and plans, and I help him come up with lots of ideas for how to make things happen."

But it isn't merely just a nice way to talk to his son. Lopez uses nexting to check in with his son to see how he is feeling about his future. Lopez says, "When he is feeling positive, his mom Alli and I do our best to 'fluff him up' even more. We know the emotional lift helps him think about ways to make his performance better, the best it can be. When we see that he is nervous or fearful, we try to figure out why, and whether we need to intervene or let him work it out." But Lopez is also quick to point out that he never offers quick fixes or automatic cheerleading tactics. Instead he believes the process of nexting helps his son realistically address the inevitable challenges everyone goes through on the way to achieving their goals and dreams. Ultimately, Lopez teaches that nexting helps us each experience more hope in the world.

More Than Just Common Sense

Although nexting sounds like good common sense, there is actually growing science in the area of positive psychology to back it up. Author Shawn Achor in his book *The Happiness Advantage* cites a study in which people who just *thought about* watching their favorite movies actually raised their endorphin levels by 27%. He says, "Anticipating future rewards can actually light up the pleasure centers in your brain as much as the actual reward will."

Alex Lickerman, M.D. and author, agrees. He says, "...anticipating something pleasant seems to have almost unequaled power to make our present glow." In fact, as Lickerman admits, "Anticipatory joy is often greater than the joy brought to us by experiencing the very things we anticipate." Lickerman is so convinced that this anticipatory joy is a good thing that he says, "Anticipatory pleasure is so important to my sense of well-being, in fact, that I now plan my life in such a way that I almost always have something to look forward to."

Probably the most recognizable version of nexting happens when any of us plan a vacation. Called "vacation anticipation," a study done in the Netherlands and published in the journal **Applied Research in Quality of Life** reports that the biggest boost of a person's happiness levels occurs in the eight weeks leading up to a vacation. And while the trip itself is usually a happy experience, shortly after returning the vacationers didn't feel any happier than those who had never taken a trip at all. Interestingly enough, the length of the trip didn't seem to increase happiness levels at all. Based on the data, study authors suggest that shorter and more frequent trips will make us happier than one long vacation once a year.

In addition, a research study done at the University of London by A.K. McLeod and C. Conway in 2005, concluded that subjects with expectations of future positive experiences were more likely to measure higher on a scale of subjective well-being. Basically, those who anticipated the future in a positive way experienced a larger social network (more friends), had a high number of steps in plans to achieve goals and even had a slightly higher household income. These are all good reasons to keep nexting for sure!

And let's not forget the power of nexting in the medical field. A study in 2011 entitled, "The Effect of Treatment Expectation on Drug Efficacy: the Analgesic Benefit of the Opioid Remifentanil," confirms what many of us have suspected for some time. It reports: "On the basis of subjective and objective evidence, we contend that an individual's expectation of a drug's effect critically influences its therapeutic efficacy and that regulatory brain mechanisms differ as a function of expectancy. We propose that it may be necessary to integrate patients' beliefs and expectations into drug treatment regimes alongside traditional considerations in order to optimize treatment outcomes." In other words, what you *next* about your medication and your treatment will influence the outcome of your healing. Wow!

I think most of us know on some level that nexting is a great way to focus on creating a more positive future. Unfortunately, I also think many of us forget this simple practice to give ourselves a "wellbeing boost" no matter what we are experiencing in our lives.

Nexting actually targets our thinking in a way that activates certain parts of our brain. As Tali Sharot, author of **The Optimism Bias** says, "A brain that doesn't expect good results lacks a signal telling it, 'Take notice — wrong answer!'" These brains will fail to learn from their mistakes and are less likely to improve over time. Expectations become self-fulfilling by altering our performance and actions, which ultimately affects what happens in the future."

But What About The Power Of Now?

Okay, I can hear all the Eckhart Tolle fans asking, "What about living in the now?" From my viewpoint, it is similar to the paradox of the yin and yang, the both/and, or a Zen Koan. While I'll admit that it can be problematic to mentally live only in the future, my life experience proves that I can live quite happily in the now and also anticipate the future with great pleasure. I personally like how Abraham-Hicks says repeatedly, "Feel happy with what is, and eagerness for what is to come."

As many people who know me personally know, I am quite a planner—especially when it comes to planning my vacations. Through the years I've had quite a few people criticize this quality saying I lack spontaneity or that I miss the experience of wonderment when I travel. I think nexting proves how very wrong that criticism is. In fact, because I "next" my travel plans so thoroughly and enjoyably, I am actually boosting my happiness factor for a much longer period of time than most people.

From all I read and from my own direct experience, I think it's safe to say that those of us who are able to "next" a positive future on a regular basis have an advantage. Indeed, to repeat what Dr. Lickerman says, "…anticipating something pleasant seems to have almost unequaled power to make our present glow." The SMART news is that this is something every single one of us can start doing today. So what are you nexting right now?

Chapter Five

Be-Good Or Get-Better? Your Choice Says A Lot About You

"Optimists are right. So are pessimists. It's
up to you to choose which you will be."
~Harvey Mackay

A couple of months ago I received a recommendation on Amazon that caught my eye. The title was ***Succeed—How We Can Reach Our Goals*** by Heidi Grant Halvorson, Ph.D. Frankly, the title didn't impress me much. Haven't we all read too many books that claim the same thing, only to nod in agreement while stifling a yawn? What hooked me instead were the reviews. Dozens of reviewers said, "It's a smart, fun, highly practical look at what we 'scientifically' know about setting and achieving goals." For those of us who enjoy learning why people do what they do (or don't do what they should do), this book backs up its claims with scientific research. And while the pursuit of goals is the focus of the book, it is done in terms of Behavior Psychology and research.

In fact, a key strategy to learning how a person pursues a goal is to discover whether they like to "Be-Good" or "Get-Better". That choice says a lot about us and often determines whether or not we eventually succeed.

So, what's the difference? A person with a Be-Good mindset approaches a goal with the intention of letting others know that they have the ability to do what is being asked of them and that all they have to do is prove it. A person with a Get-Better mindset is focused on developing their abilities and learning new skills. As Halvorson says, "You can think of it as the difference between wanting to show that you *are* smart versus wanting to *get* smarter."

In many ways the Be-Good and the Get-Better mindset mirrors the perspective of Carol Dweck in her work on the "fixed" versus the "growth" mindset. That work tells me that it is important to remember that a person can either perceive their abilities as being set from birth, and that those abilities need only to be demonstrated (fixed) –or they can see those abilities as something flexible that can be developed and enhanced (growth). Whichever mindset people choose can often determine their success and happiness during their lifetime.

Going further, Halvorson explains in detail how a Be-Good perspective differs from a Get-Better perspective in terms of achieving goals in day-to-day life. As the term Be-Good implies, a primary focus of a person with this intention is to constantly look outside themselves to confirm their success. Comparison is therefore a bigger problem because a Be-Gooder always needs to check their performance with everyone else to see how they size up. Meanwhile, someone with a Get-Better perspective is more into self-awareness and personal progress as they proceed along the path of change. Unfortunately, because I frequently struggled to be the "good daughter, good wife, good person" as a young woman, the limitations of the Be-Good mindset were all too familiar.

One of the more interesting ways to compare these two perspectives is in the terms of birth-order. In research by Halvorson, firstborn siblings were "significantly" more likely to have Get-Better perspective using self-referenced standards. On the other hand, second-born children were more likely to pursue Be-Good goals with a tendency to compare their performance to others. Again, as a second born sibling, my tendency towards the Be-Good attitude was set early on.

More insight on this mindset comes from the student achievement studies that compare Asian students with American students in terms of science and math. Since 1995 when the tests were first administered, American children have significantly been outperformed by peers in China, Korea, Singapore and Japan. Why? According to Halvorson the answer is simple, "Americans believe in ability, and East Asians believe in effort." In other words, ability is a Be-Good approach while effort is a Get-Better approach. Research of these differences show that Americans typically believe failure occurs due to lack of ability, training, luck and effort. On the other hand, Chinese mothers believe failure is mostly just "lack of effort."

Because Americans tend to place such a large emphasis on measuring abilities (i.e. standardized testing, IQ tests, etc.) we primarily emphasize Be-Good goals for our students and that is playing out on a global scale. On a personal basis I never felt I was "good" at math in school so never applied much effort. The truth was, because I never tried to expand my knowledge in math (English was so much easier), I have no idea how well I could have done if had made the effort to learn.

So how does knowing about this help us on a day-to-day basis? As Halvorson says, "goals are like lenses in a pair of glasses. The goals you pursue determine not only what you see but how you see it—the things you notice and how you interpret what happens to you." For that reason, it is very important that we recognize our mindset and figure out ways to ensure that our goals reflect what will more likely bring us closer to that which will make us happy and fulfilled.

For example, what do most students hope to get when they go to college? Chances are that if you ask any student what they want to achieve they will say that they want to get good grades. But now that we know "good" grades are the goals of a Get-Good mindset, it's easy to see how that sets us up to compare ourselves with others and to strive to prove that we are smart. Instead, a Get-Better approach gives us the option of saying our goal is to learn as much as possible about our area of study and ourselves—and to enjoy the journey along the way.

There are also a number of other striking differences between the two mindsets. A person who is focused on Be-Good can be very motivated to achieve success. It's easy to see how comparing ourselves to others can drive us to push ourselves. But research shows that while it can create excellent performances, if things become too difficult it often leads a person with that mindset to completely GIVE UP rather than continue. A person who spends his or her life striving to Be-Good feels like a failure when things get tough.

Meanwhile, people with a Get-Better mindset take difficulty in stride. They use their challenges to improve themselves and their resilience allows them to face just about any difficulty. And as said before, those with a Get-Better mindset also tend to enjoy the journey more—no matter what the goal. They aren't trying to prove anything to anyone else, only to see how far they can go. They also have fewer problems with asking others for help because again, they aren't as worried about what others think of them.

Another interesting fact is that students who spend a lot of time trying to Be-Good are more likely to get depressed than those who consistently focus on Getting-Better. And the more depressed the Be-Gooders got, the less motivated they felt. On the flip side, students with a Get-Better approach actually stayed much more motivated. As Halvorson said, "If you focus on growth instead of validation, on making progress instead of proving yourself, you are less likely to get depressed…And you are less likely to stay depressed."

While most of this information seems relatively simple, the implications are huge. As the second born in a family with three other sisters I am all too familiar with comparing myself to my siblings and the goal to "be good" as much as possible. In school I attempted to prove myself with good grades and validate myself with good behavior. I never once remember being told to enjoy the journey and to appreciate and enjoy my desire to learn for the sake of learning.

The good news is that the Be-Good and the Get-Better perspectives are mindsets that can be changed as we go—and there are dozens of benefits to the process. The first step is to remember that we do have the choice. The second is to keep in mind that a good life is about the journey rather than the destination. Next, if we can stop comparing ourselves to others and trying to validate our very existence, we will learn to appreciate the unique character that we are. Beyond that, by accepting that your abilities are tied to the effort you put forth rather than your fixed talents, you will be able to accomplish so much more than otherwise. Furthermore, challenges will no longer seem as threatening; they become mere stepping-stones to more growth. Finally, when we discover that mistakes don't make us a failure, we can learn to appreciate our newfound skills and gain valuable information.

I accept that I have spent too much of my life in pursuit of Be-Good goals. Fortunately, I now know how SMART it is to realize that every one of us can grow and change anything that no longer serves us. And yes, that's a sure way to succeed!

Chapter Six

Seven Mental Illusions That Influence Our Everyday Thinking

"The way we habitually think of our surroundings and ourselves creates the worlds that each of us inhabit."
~Charles Duhigg

A big part of Living SMART 365 is staying conscious, awake and aware. In fact, the majority of us like to believe that's what we do most of the time. But after reading the book, ***"Thinking Fast & Slow"*** by Daniel Kahneman, I've discovered that I am seldom as awake and aware as I think I am. In fact, far too often I frame most of my decisions like a lot of you—in the easiest and most comfortable ways possible. Fortunately, now that I have a better understanding of how human thinking and decision-making works, I can be more awake and conscious about some of the most routine illusions that befall us all.

So, what are some of the biggest mental illusions that all of us fall victim to, and how do they affect our individual realities? The biggest by far is that our minds strive to achieve coherence and understanding no matter what we face. In other words, we can (and do) rationalize and justify just about anything we want if it suits the story of meaning we have accepted. Plus, because our minds labor towards "sense-making" at every waking second, we frequently see the world as more tidy, simple, predictable and coherent than it often is. More times than not, we believe just about anything to avoid uncertainty or confusion. We constantly make judgments quickly, stereotype, and jump to conclusions without even being aware we are doing the jumping. Even worse, we don't like to be wrong, and we'll avoid even trying to win in order not to lose. While some of these mental processes are certainly valuable and save a lot of time, we error if we use them without awareness. And guess what? Like it or not, we think in these ways much of the time.

Here are seven mental illusions to watch out for on a daily basis:

1) **The Halo Effect**. When you think someone is attractive—or like and agree with what they say, you will automatically give them more credibility than otherwise. You will believe most of what they say and overlook things (like the truth!) or ignore anyone that disagrees with them. While there is no question that we all do this, we usually just do it without awareness. The opposite is also true. If you don't like the way someone looks, or you don't like them for any reason whatsoever—you'll distrust what they say and be suspicious—regardless of whether they are telling the truth or not. Remember, we ALL

do this ALL the time.

2) WYSIATI—What You See Is All There Is! Because we want to make sense of our experiences, WE DON'T EVEN SEE WHAT DOESN'T FIT OUR PICTURE OF REALITY. This is pretty scary when you realize that people who don't want to believe something—politically, religiously, and educationally—can't hear or see an opposing view. If you have a hard time grasping a different point of view—that's probably because you don't want to! Again, the reach of this illusion is huge and yes, we all do it all the time.

3) The Availability Bias. Because our minds seek coherence and compatibility, we naturally gravitate to ideas, suggestions and meanings that we have heard or believed before. This bias is also strong with whatever attracts your attention including the latest dramatic events on the nightly news, or the most notorious Hollywood scandal. Because these events are so vivid, they stand out and appear bigger and more relevant than do other experiences in your life—and we frequently make choices accordingly.

Studies show that unless we are conscious, we will make choices believing something looks more correct when it is in **bold type,** when we read it more than once somewhere, or even if we heard it in a commercial. Understand? We just about always are blinded by our natural tendencies toward what we have seen or heard before. Don't believe me? Do you ever purchase popular name brands even if a better and cheaper one is available?

4) Framing Affects Our Stories. As story-making beings, we tend to put a frame around everything we believe. That frame helps us keep things in context—but it can work against us. For example, advertisers know that if they present certain information one way vs. another they can often motivate us without our knowing about it. The most amazing example of this is the fact that in some countries the rate of organ donation is almost 100%! In other countries, like the U.S., the rate of organ donation is very low. This low rate is attributed to the fact that people must "opt-in" and consciously decide to become organ donors when getting their driver's licenses. In other countries where participation is nearly 100%, they are required instead to choose to "opt-out" or they are automatically enrolled. Because people nearly always take THE EASY ROUTE, and retailers and others know that about us, they frame the process in a way that gives them what they want—and most of us automatically comply.

5) The Illusion Of Understanding. We are drawn to stories that are simple to understand, and concrete rather than abstract. And because we like to make sense of everything— our view of the past is frequently just a story we have created to understand what happened within our worldview. This "hindsight bias" goes so far that it actually makes it very difficult for us to even recall what we used to believe before we changed our mind. Plus, as Kahneman explained, "The illusion that we understand the past fosters overconfidence in our ability to predict the future."

6) The illusion Of validity And skill. Because so many of these mental biases work together to create our understanding and beliefs, it is difficult to unravel why we actually believe what we do. In fact, in our desire to maintain coherence we tend to overestimate skill (and ignore concrete evidence) if it fits within the stories we have created. For example, we so want to believe that professionals know what they are doing, and are working for our benefit, that we often ignore choices that should never ever be turned over to others—like our health, finances and relationships.

7) The Optimistic Bias. This is a bias I never thought I would want to watch out for—but it is rampant in our culture and important to know. This bias says that we tend to overestimate our chances at success and underestimate our chances at failure. A large part of our estimations come from our desire to believe that when we are in charge we know enough to be in control. Why do people go into a business with no chance to succeed? Why do most teenagers believe they are going to grow up to be the next superstar? Why do criminals think they will never get caught? This bias, along with the illusion of skill, tends to make us ignore anything that stands in the way of our desires. Of course, I'm not giving up this bias altogether—but I do want to be aware of it before making any important decision.

Believe it or not, these aren't all the illusions and biases described in this book, just the ones I think are the most important to remember. As a person who believes that our lives and experiences are created as a result of our thinking and consciousness, this information is vital. That's because if we do "get to make it up," then knowing what we are using to create our worldview can definitely impact the outcome. More than anything, this book reminds me that it is challenging to stay conscious, awake and aware, and that real thinking requires effort. While not everyone is ready to take on that challenge, the quality of our life depends on it.

Chapter Seven

Going Beyond Trauma And Pain To Reveal Post Traumatic Growth (PTG)

"Nearly anything is possible.... even when a circumstance can't be changed, we can alter our perception of it." ~Amy Purdy

Most of us are familiar with the idea that trauma, especially extreme trauma like war, rape or life-threatening illness, can lead to a condition called PTSD (post-traumatic-stress-syndrome.) But what many might not realize is that some people who have experienced those extreme tragedies not only learn to cope and adapt but actually manage to thrive. Called Post-Traumatic-Growth (PTG) these resilient people appear to be both "antifragile" and "stress inoculated." Best of all, this mindset allows them to do better than "bounce back" from whatever trauma they have experienced, and to "bounce forward" in strong and meaningful ways. Perhaps the SMARTest thing any of us can do would be to cultivate the possibility of PTG into our everyday lives so that we adjust, learn and create something new and better in the days ahead.

The label Post Traumatic Growth (PTG) first appeared in 1995 out of the work of a psychologist named Dr. Richard Tedeschi from the University of North Carolina. Tedeschi's work focused on the parents who had children who died from either disease or accident. Attempting to understand how parents might cope with such profound loss, he discovered some people not only turned it around, they used their grief to do something transformative for themselves and others. What he observed was that while the process of growth does not diminish or eliminate the pain of loss and tragedy, positive gains are possible in spite of the most shattering heartbreak.

On the flipside, PTSD first applied to veterans of the Vietnam War. It is estimated that up to 30% of those who saw action in Vietnam and other wars suffer from the affliction. Since that time, it has been determined that anyone who survives any catastrophic event, natural disaster, or acts of violence and pain are potential victims to the symptoms. Those symptoms include: flashbacks, nightmares, high levels of anxiety and depression, substance abuse and an inability to cope with the trauma.

According to the VA Administration in Nebraska, up to 7.8% of the U.S. population will experience PTSD during some time in their life. However, research shows that most people are resilient overall. Estimates say that while 50-60% of North Americans will experience different traumas in their lives, only 5-10% will ever develop symptoms of PTSD.

So, is PTG just another name for resiliency? Not really. PTG utilizes the experience, no matter how traumatic, and allows a person to arrive at a new and more beneficial understanding of themselves and their lives. Resilience, on the other hand, allows a person to overcome challenges but basically remain the same after the experience has been resolved in one manner or another. Resilience requires useful coping strategies, where PTG requires a change of consciousness or transformation. In other words, the thriving of PTG includes not only resiliency but an enhanced improvement in the quality of life following the trauma.

What Benefits Come From PTG?

There are at least five benefits that show up in a person who experiences PTG. They are:

- Greater appreciation of life;

- Changed sense of priorities, new possibilities;

- Warmer, more intimate relationships;

- Greater self-confidence and personal strength;

- Enhanced spirituality;

Remember, no one is suggesting that the answer to trauma or extreme stress is to pretend it away or lay blame on another for not moving past the experience. And it is never valid to try to convince another that the trauma or the hardships they have endured are a good thing. But merely knowing that PTG is available and that the possibility that something good can result from the struggle, can be very beneficial. Research has proven that people who experienced everything from the violence of terrorism to the trauma of breast cancer have managed to find positive psychological growth through PTG.

Predictors of PTG

But what type of person normally experiences PTG? Clearly, much of the response has to do with a person's mindset and perceptions. But beyond that, research points out that the following are usually aspects of the person's personality.

- Extraversion;

- Openness to experiences;

- A spiritual belief;

- Good social support;

- Acceptance coping…. the ability to accept situations which cannot be changed;

Research indicates that of these five, scientists consider the first two to be the most important.

Finding PTG On Our Own

Obviously, if a person is suffering from PTSD along with related symptoms they should seek out competent mental health aid. But what about the rest of us? Anyone who is feeling overwhelmed, helpless, hopeless and deeply stressed would benefit from realizing that no matter how traumatic, it is possible that something good can come from the experience. Not only can we find something beneficial out of any stress, we ourselves can become stronger and more empowered to meet the future. So how can we do that?

Author and educator Shawn Achor suggests that we consider several different strategies. The first is to attempt to reinterpret the situation in a more positive way. By using our imagination and learning to describe the event in a more positive way, we can be empowered. He also suggests that we stay as optimistic as possible. In addition, he suggests that we should meet the situation head-on (rather than deny or avoid it) as much as we are able. Achor says, "It appears that it is not the type of event per se that influences posttraumatic growth, but rather the subjective experience of the event." He goes on to say, "Things do not necessarily happen for the best, but some people are able to make the best out of things that happen."

Achor also describes two other techniques that hold great power to transform our life. The first is to "change your counterpoint." He uses the question: "If you were in a bank with 50 other people and some robbers came in and shot you in the arm, how would you describe the event?" Obviously, most people would see the trauma, resent the experience, and feel victimized. On the other hand, Shawn says that it is equally possible for you to say, "Wow, that could have been so much worse! I feel so fortunate to be alive." Or, "There were 50 people in that bank and I was the only one that took a bullet. I'm lucky to be alive to tell the tale." Remember, we are the people choosing the "alternate-fact." While our alternate-fact doesn't change the truth, it does describe it from a different perspective.

The other technique Achor describes is to change our "explanatory style". Whenever we communicate our experiences to others, we have a style uniquely ours. Some of our stories highlight the good and share that narrative. Others pick out everything that is wrong or bad and share that. According to Achor, there are studies that show that our "explanatory style—how we choose to explain the nature of past events—has a crucial impact on our happiness and future success." Obviously, our explanatory style can be sculpted so that it aids in PTG.

At the same time, Jim Rendon, author of the book, ***Upside—The New Science of Post Traumatic Growth*** believes that achieving a PTG mindset is fairly natural to us all. He says in his book, "In study after study, research shows that about half or more of trauma survivors report positive change as a result of their experience," Rendon writes. "...Every time I talk to one of these people in my reporting — someone who has totally altered his life, his sense of self, someone who says he is thankful for what most of us would consider a terrible tragedy — I am thrilled and amazed," he continues. "What an exceptional person, I think. And then I remember all of the others who have told me similar stories. This kind of miraculous transformation, it turns out, is hardly unusual. The potential for such inspiring change lives inside most people."

Several years ago I was in a motorcycle accident and broke my left arm and injured that shoulder requiring surgery. I wasn't able to use my left arm for several weeks afterward and kept it in a sling to keep it still. When I finally started physical therapy, my arm was so weak and painful I couldn't even crawl-the-wall. And while I had to take it slow, I also knew it was necessary to keep going. Not only did I learn that anything we don't use regularly or develop naturally, becomes weaker as days go by. I also discovered that my broken left arm, once healed, was now much stronger than my right, never-broken, arm would ever be.

While my experience is nothing compared to the trauma that some people experience, I think remembering that just like my arm, anything we hide away or try to protect will never recover until we take the time to rehabilitate it. By the same token, once we have worked through our recovery, we can be stronger because of the experience. Perhaps even better, we can begin to see the world as a more interconnected whole where we have an important part to play.

When you think about it, the implications of PTG also extend to experiences on a global, national and regional scale. Depending on which side of the political pendulum you inhabit, you might be traumatized by current events. While experiences can appear potentially catastrophic, holding the belief that the potential for positive transformation exists can be empowering. Remember, regardless of the trauma, studies show that for some people, the worst possible experience turned out to be the best thing that ever could have happened.

Clearly, none of us consciously seeks trauma in order to experience growth or to become stronger or wiser. And learning about PTG won't stop it from happening. But should trauma infect us at any time in our lives, the possibility always exists to create positive change. Regardless of what happens in the world, our country, on Facebook, or our own back yard, it is SMART to remember that Post Traumatic Growth could lead to the transformation we all want to see happen.

Chapter Eight

Letting Go Of The Need To Be Right

*"The greatest revolution of our generation is
the discovery that human beings, by
changing the inner attitudes of their minds,
can change the outer aspects of their lives."*
~William James

I think if you ask most people, they will agree that being happy is more important than being right. But if that's true, why do so many of us, me included, frequently choose the opposite? For the most part, we hang on to our ideas, beliefs and perceptions as though our lives depended upon them. Even when it is a relatively minor point like what toothpaste to buy, many of us will clutch our opinions like dogs with a bone. Unfortunately, it is easy to see that the more we insist we are right, the more we alienate others, frustrate ourselves, stymie our growth, restrict our ability to change and cut ourselves off from our true nature. So, I decided to take a look in the mirror and do my best to let go of being so attached to being right—starting now.

Where does it begin? I think most of us (at least in Western cultures) learned somewhere in childhood that being right was a good way to get love, attention and reward. Instead of encouraging us to enjoy the process of learning, the majority of our school systems are set up so that being right is "good," and being wrong is "bad." At some point, I learned that when I had the correct answer to my teacher's questions, I stood out in a positive way. If I was mistaken or simply didn't know, I was ignored or even ridiculed. We all were. That's why it didn't take most of us long to realize that being right was a path to love, acceptance and attention.

It only gets worse as we age. If we work hard to absorb the "right" knowledge and then define ourselves as someone who "knows" such things, we get more and more attached to what we know as "right". Along the way we begin connecting our identity, our sense of safety, meaning and our ability to control the unexpected, as it merges with our knowing of what's right as opposed to anything that doesn't fit our mold.

Of course, the more solidified our thinking becomes, the more difficult it is for us to even be aware of what we are doing. As Kathryn Schultz, author of **BEING WRONG** says, we all fall victim to "error blindness." In other words, we can't see anything that doesn't fit into our perception of the world and ourselves. As Schultz goes on to say, "The miracle of your mind isn't that you can see the world as it is—but that you can see the world as it ISN'T." And we all do this every day all the time. The biggest problem of course is that we forget we are literally "making things up" and insist that others agree with us.

How do we continue to reinforce our own rightness? Shultz explains it by saying that we first confront anyone who refuses to believe what we've come to think of as fact, by believing they are just ignorant. Surely if they had the same facts they would agree we are right? Then, if THEY don't change and still don't recognize our "rightness," we begin to think of them as idiots. Finally, if they still insist on believing something different from what we know to be right and true, then we surrender to the idea that they are just plain evil. Admit it. Chances are good you've thought those things too.

That reminds me of a story I heard from a friend. My friend who I'll call Nancy was at the airport before her flight when it was announced that her flight would be delayed. Trying to make the best of it, Nancy went to the airport store and purchased a water and a small bag of Famous Amos Chocolate Chip Cookies. She jammed them in her oversized purse and then went and found a seat, got settled with a book, and began reading.

Almost immediately a man came and sat right next to her in spite of the fact there were plenty of other seats nearby. Nancy did her best to just ignore him and kept on reading. But to her amazement, the man grabbed her bag of Famous Amos cookies sitting on the ledge between their chairs, opened the bag and started to pull one out. Seeing her surprised look, the man actually paused, extended the bag in her direction, and offered her one of her own cookies!

Nancy didn't trust herself enough to say anything because she was so riled up. So pursing her lips, Nancy quickly reached into the bag, grabbed one of HER cookies and immediately returned to reading her book as she angrily munched away. From the corner of her eye she could see the man shrug and then grab his own cookie before gazing out at the throngs of people passing by. Before long, he reached back into the bag, pulled out another cookie for himself and once again extended the bag in her direction as an offering. And so it went without a word between them. One by one they both ate through her bag of cookies—her seething with indignation and him remaining nonchalantly calm and detached. Finally, the man crumpled up the bag, nodded his head in her direction before rising and walking down the terminal.

Nancy was furious. No wonder the world was in such a bad state! Not only had a man basically stolen her cookies right in front of her, he didn't even have the courtesy to thank her for them. Realizing her anger and the cookies had made her thirsty. Nancy reached inside her bag and her hand closed around, not the bottle of water, but a bag of Famous Amos Cookies. Yep, all the time she was rigid with anger at a stranger for eating HER cookies, he was being generous, kind and gracious in spite of her obvious hostility.

Our sense of rightness does that to us. It blinds us to

what is really going on around us and convinces us that our perspective is the right one and most everyone else knows less. Many people believe that it's our "ego" that wants us to be right most of the time, and they certainly make a good point. But I'm starting to believe that it just might be my ego trying to protect and keep me safe in an uncertain world. After all, if I am right about most everything, I'm also in control and bad things won't happen to me, right? Sorry! Even if it were possible to be so right that nothing bad ever happened to anyone, that would have worked for someone by now. But to make matters worse, we just keep trying to be right until it becomes such a habit that we aren't even aware of it anymore.

Not only does thinking we are right NOT keep us safe from uncertainty, it also carries a few other downsides. The most obvious problem is we become extremely inflexible and close-minded. When we are afraid to be wrong or make mistakes we never try anything new and become calcified. We are terrible listeners, we are less creative, less happy, and much, much less fun to be around. Don't we all know someone who thinks they know everything there is to know about every subject?

Let's face it—most of us are terrified by not knowing. We've arrived at a place in our lives where we are deeply attached to what we think we know. Then the more successful we've been at it, it's likely we are more attached to it than ever before. Having someone disagree with us, or admitting that someone else knows more, asks us to realize that we don't really know as much as we think we do.

In some ways wanting to be "right" is just another case of perfectionism. Again, it's about feeling safe, in control and in charge of what's going on around you. And as Brene Brown says, "Perfectionism is a defensive move. It is the belief that if we do things perfectly and look perfect, we can minimize or avoid the pain of blame, judgment and shame." Wanting to be right and have others agree with us, like perfectionism, "…is, at its core, about trying to earn approval."

I'll admit it again—I like to be right. But now that I know much of that feeling is really an attempt to feel safe, in control and win approval from others, I can watch out for it more consciously. Then, next time I catch myself asserting myself defensively, I'm going to pause, take a breath and look at what belief or perspective within me is being challenged, what I'm afraid of or if something within me needs to change. Only with such a SMART awareness and desire, can we ever know we are okay whether or not anyone else agrees with us or thinks we're "right."

Chapter Nine

Five Choices Taught By Caroline Myss That Lead To Healing & Better Health

"Who you become as a person is up to you—
up to your imagination, your will, your
determination, your choices." ~ *Maria Shriver*

Ever since reading ***Why People Don't Heal—And How They Can*** by Caroline Myss, Ph.D. back in the late 1990s I have been a fan. No matter how many times I read her work, or listen to a lecture she gives, I am always inspired. Myss continually fills in the blanks in many of my thoughts about how to stay healthy and happy from a psychological and spiritual perspective that is often absent in so many conversations. This last week I found a recent TED Talk she gave at the Findhorn Foundation. In this short talk she presents five choices that she has observed in her long career that she finds essential to living a long and healthy life. Surprisingly so—it isn't the big choices that make the real difference, it's those little daily ones that matter.

In case you aren't familiar with Myss, she is a five-time **New York Times** bestselling author and renowned speaker in the fields of human consciousness, spirituality and mysticism, health, energy medicine and the science of medical intuition. Certainly, one of the more interesting aspects of her work is the fact that she is medically intuitive. In other words, she can do a "reading" on a person who is facing health issues and offer a psychological, emotional and/or spiritual explanation for why that person has become ill. After years of working with people from this energetic perspective, Myss has learned to identify a variety of common themes that appear to be at the root of many mental and emotional blocks to becoming healthy and well.

Central to her work is the idea that we are all energetic beings—and that our health exists within the combination of our physical, mental, emotional and spiritual wholeness. In other words, illness does not just descend upon a person from nowhere. To Myss, everything is connected. Beyond that, as she says, "We need to create health every day and all the time, and we need to do so consciously."

Obviously, this mixture of internal and external influence requires deep thinking and exploration. However, during the recent lecture I heard, Myss says most of it boils down to our choices. According to Myss, "Choice is a fundamental power of the human experience." But again, these aren't the big things like who to marry, when to marry or should you buy a house or go to college. Instead, these choices are those subtle decisions we make each and every day when we wake up and go about our day. According to Myss, the big five we need to consciously answer every day are:

1) The decision to live with integrity. In other words, learn to walk your talk. Besides always telling the truth, this also means not compromising ourselves to keep the peace or to get others to love or like us. It also asks us not to ask others to compromise themselves to please us. Myss says, "Liars don't heal." We must be truthful with others and ourselves. And Myss believes that what we eat or how much we exercise matters far less than our honesty. It's not about being a good person—it is about being true to ourselves.

2) Choosing to share our wisdom rather than our pain. What do we want to pass on? What is it that we want to share with others on a daily basis? Myss believes the path to healing is one where we share the wisdom we've learned in every experience—rather than the suffering. But make no mistake, Myss recognizes that we all have times of pain and grief—but we can still make that choice. She suggests we let go of wanting life to be fair. And she also doesn't believe it is helpful to know why something happened. Just let it go. Some of the grief and injuries that have happened to people are truly horrible and nothing can ever make the pain go away. But ultimately it is not about denying the tragedies. Instead it is looking it in the face and saying, "This will never defeat me." She says we can all choose between wisdom and woe.

3) The choice to take risks. Don't wait for proof. Don't ask for everything to be clear or easy. Take risks. Refuse to slide into regretful living. Most of the time we hold back on decisions that seem risky because we fear being humiliated by failure or by what others think. Myss says, "Never look backward for guidance." But especially, when you don't know what to do next, do not go to what you once were or what used to exist. We weaken ourselves by looking backward. Instead, exist in the "newness" of possibility.

4) Choose new words. A lover of words, Myss considers words powerful. Start paying attention to the words you say to others but most especially the words you say to yourself. She strongly advises us to never ignore the power of the vocabulary we use. Myss recalls saying to a woman who came to her searching for answers to why healing eluded her. Myss told her, "Your vocabulary is so toxic that the vibration of your neurology includes thoughts, includes frequencies, that are so toxic that even if you do visualization, it is offset by a vocabulary that is organically so negative...I don't care what your visualization is...If I had to rate your vocabulary it is fundamentally hostile toward everything you see, toward everyone, and toward yourself. You get up in the morning and you are hostile, your first thoughts are angry, you see your life as not enough, you see others as not enough. Your first reaction to everything is critical."

Clearly, any of us would do well to avoid words that promote those thoughts or reactions. Of particular note, Myss strongly suggests we avoid three powerful words: 1) blame, 2) deserve, 3) entitled. She says, "If you could extricate those three words from your head, you have no idea how much better you would feel." Blaming others for anything takes you out of the present and puts toxic perceptions inside of you.

5) Choose to get up every day and bless your day. Be happy to be alive and refuse to base your gratitude on what you have or how you feel—just be grateful because *you are.* Celebrate each day as a unique moment never to be repeated. This choice alone should take all bitterness out of our hearts and allow us to see the present with gratitude.

Regardless of whether you believe that Myss has the ability to diagnose illness, along with the thoughts and energy that are blocking a person's healing, it is hard to argue with her perspective on choice. And while she strongly urges everyone to take full responsibility for their health and circumstances, including those with all types of illness, she doesn't do it to make people feel guilty. Instead she believes that only through total responsibility do we retain the ability to be fully empowered to take action and make a change.

Myss believes that our tiniest choices have infinite consequences and the choices we make in the privacy of our own company have the ability to heal and fully empower us. Perhaps the SMART option is to stay open to the possibility and as always, stay grateful for yet another day of life.

Chapter Ten

Argue For Your Limitations & They Are Yours— Another Case of Motivational Reasoning

"You'll see it when you believe it." ~*Wayne Dyer*

Have you ever heard the statement, "Argue for your limitations, and they're yours"? In case you're wondering, that quote comes from a book written by Richard Bach entitled, ***Illusions: The Adventures of a Reluctant Messiah.*** When I first read it years ago I thought I knew what it meant. What's interesting is that I seem to need to learn that lesson over and over again.

Limitations, of course, are any excuses I use to hold myself back and not live the life I dream of living. Limitations are also the rationalizations we all use for doing or not doing something, or believing or not believing just about anything. The big problem is that limitations seem so *real* that we often think we have no choice but to believe them. Fortunately, there is now scientific proof that much of what is going on in our minds are stories we tell ourselves—that may or may not be, true. So if we are making up stories as we go along—why on earth would we invent stories that limit us and hold us back?

I think I do it, *we* do it, because we all forget that our conscious thoughts are largely a collection of perceptions, expectations, judgments and fantasy—not necessarily the truth. Author Leonard Mlodinow says in his book, **Subliminal—How Your Unconscious Mind Rules Your Behavior** "…the subtlety of our reasoning mechanisms allows us to maintain our illusions of objectivity even while viewing our world through a biased lens." Mlodinow goes on to say, *"We choose the facts we want to believe."*

A big part of this phenomenon is a mental process called "motivated reasoning." Similar to a term called "confirmation bias" where we give unequal weight to any concept we already believe; motivated reasoning takes it to the next level because it involves our emotions. According to the **Skeptic's Dictionary** an online resource, "Motivated reasoning leads people to confirm what they already believe, while ignoring contrary data. But it also drives people to develop elaborate rationalizations to justify holding beliefs that logic and evidence have shown to be wrong." Motivated reasoning is an emotional survival skill that is so ingrained and instinctual that it operates automatically when confronted with new, alarming or conflicting information.

University of Virginia psychologist Jonathan Haidt explains the emotional urge rising from motivated reasoning as the difference between a scientist and a lawyer. Most of us believe that when we are thinking, planning and arriving at conclusions we are like scientists gathering data and logically arriving at the highest, best and most truthful answer. Instead, we are actually more like lawyers—we begin with a foregone conclusion in mind and then do our best to convince others (and ourselves) that all the *real* evidence supports that predetermined conclusion. But our "inner attorney" doesn't stop there–he/she will actually aggressively discredit any and all evidence that doesn't support that set conclusion. As Mlodinow says in his book, "The brain is a decent scientist but an absolutely *outstanding* lawyer."

In other words, if we *really* want to believe we can or can't do something—there is no one or no facts, no matter how logical or well researched, which can make us believe it! Argue for your limitations and they're yours. As Mlodinow says, "Because motivated reasoning is unconscious, people's claims that they are unaffected by bias or self-interest can be sincere, even as they make decisions that are in reality self-serving." Obviously we can use motivated reasoning to think we know everything there is to know about something or we can use it to rationalize anything we don't want to or can't imagine doing in our lives.

Huge examples of the illusion of motivated reasoning exist on the national scale. For example, remember the Radio

Doomsday Church that was convinced the world was going to end on May 21st, 2009? While most Americans laughed at their apocalyptic message, 350 of them paid roughly $23,000 each to buy a place in a bunker so they would survive the end of the world. No amount of facts could persuade them otherwise. Crazy? In a more modern example, even though the National Academy of Sciences, the American Association for the Advancement of Science, the American Geophysical Union, the American Meteorological Society and 97% to 98% of climate experts around the world have concluded that human activity is largely responsible for Climate Change, more than half the people in the United States have managed to convince themselves that the science of global warming is not settled. Motivated reasoning works for or against us—and because it is tied to emotion, anything that brings up our fears and insecurities becomes even more suspect.

That's why motivated reasoning is behind the excuses a person will give for staying with a partner who is unfaithful or abusive. It also motivates the rationalization that people use to stay stuck in a job they hate, put up with people or family that are insulting, or stay in any situation that is clearly not in their best interest. Every one of us is deeply invested in our identity and protecting our sense of self, and because of that, if anyone tries to convince someone else of their bias, it can and often does backfire so that he or she grasps their wrong views even more tenaciously. Another interesting fact is that the intelligence and education of a person doesn't help them see through their motivated reasoning to the truth. Instead, the more education or intelligence the person resisting the new information has, the more sophisticated the rationalizations and counterarguments become.

Want someone you care about to hear your side of the story or hear your advice? Then the best way to *avoid* kicking in his or her motivated reasoning is to make sure you present it to them in a context that doesn't trigger a defensive, emotional reaction. According to Dan Kahan, you don't lead with the facts in order to convince, you lead with values—so as to give the facts a fighting chance.

I don't know what excuses you routinely use to keep you from doing what you dream of doing or becoming. Shoot, I can barely get clear of my own. What I now know is that we need to continually challenge what we believe to be true and to be willing to be wrong regarding just about everything we hold dear. It is also SMART for us to attempt to listen to the messages we hear from others—not defensively or reactionary—but to honestly listen to determine if what they are saying is something that will benefit us from knowing about ourselves.

What it comes down to is the realization that motivated reasoning makes all our certainties suspect. If we truly want to learn to live our dreams, find and follow our purpose, and understand ourselves, then looking at those things we defend and argue about just might be the place to start. It's SMART to remember that whatever limitations we argue for—we own!

Chapter Eleven

Not My Monkey—Not My Circus

"Nobody but you is responsible for your life. It doesn't matter what your mama did; it doesn't matter what your daddy didn't do. You are responsible for your life. … You are responsible for the energy that you create for yourself, and you're responsible for the energy that you bring to others." ~Oprah

I'm not sure why but I tend to be almost fanatical about my commitments. If I say I'm going to do something, come hell or high water, I'll do it. For the most part this quality has served me very well. However, sometimes this obsession gets me in trouble. That usually happens when the edges of my commitment get fuzzy with the actions or non-actions of others. Before I know it, I'm sucked into involvement and drama that is not of my doing, and often not even in my control. That's why the Polish proverb, "Not my monkey, not my circus," has become a valuable mantra for my life.

I first saw this phrase on Facebook. I know not everyone is happy with Facebook policies and some of the silliness we see there. But jewels like this statement pop up every now and then and make the experience valuable. I've also seen the quote as, "Not my circus. Not my monkeys." But I prefer to put the monkey first because I usually get involved with the people first and then find myself drawn into their circus. From now on I want to steer clear of both.

Need an example? A few years ago I agreed to volunteer for a local organization. Volunteering meant a significant commitment of my time and energy, but because I agreed to do it, I jumped in feet first. Thankfully, the return on my "gift" has rewarded me in many ways. Then a year ago I saw a need in the organization and volunteered to fill that beyond my previous commitment. Unfortunately, I underestimated the increased commitment making the new position more challenging. To top it off, a woman in the leadership of the group made my work even more difficult than anticipated.

A couple of weeks ago this woman I'll call Jane phoned me in a panic telling me that she had screwed up and not checked some vital facts that affected dozens of people. She asked if I could help. In some ways, the wise answer would have been to pause and think it over before agreeing to help because this wasn't the first time this had happened. But Jane didn't stop there. Jane told me her father had just passed away and that she was critically needed to go to the aid of her sick mother. With that as an excuse, how could I not help?

The thing is, yesterday Jane called in a panic yet again. Even though I had previously spent a couple of hours unravelling her mistake, she had not communicated the information to the right person and had essentially made the problem even worse. Could I help? Thankfully I got conscious and awake enough to tell myself *what I needed to hear.* "She is not my monkey. That is NOT my circus."

Now I'm not saying that I am conscious enough to never be sucked again into someone else's drama—but I hope I am getting there. Of course, the closer to home the "drama" is, the more likely we are to think it is ours in the first place. Plus, if the drama is happening to a family member or a close friend, many of us feel that it is only right or compassionate to help whenever called upon. But when we are more compassionate to others, and neglect and abuse ourselves, is that what compassion is asking for? And at what point is that "help" more about our need for love, acceptance and approval, than it is to really offer that person what they need above all else? We need to make sure we aren't just doing it to prove our worth.

Letting go of other people's monkeys and circus is something many of us have wrestled with throughout our lives. I've always loved a Buddha story with the same theme that asks the question, "If someone offers you a gift and you refuse to accept it, who does it belong to?" According to the story, one day the Buddha was walking down the street and a man approached him and started hurtling insults and accusations at him. The Buddha calmly listened to the man until he stomped his feet, waved his arms in the air and marched off down the street.

Another man who saw the incident walked over to the Buddha and asked him, "How were you able to not respond to that man?" The Buddha merely paused and asked this new man, "If someone offers you a gift and you refuse to accept it, who does it belong to?" In other words, what the first man offered was not his monkey, not his circus.

This message is repeated over and over by others as well. Author Richard Carlson, Ph.D. said something just like it in his book, ***Don't Sweat the Small Stuff…and it's all small stuff***. Carlson reminds us that, "If someone throws you the ball, you don't have to catch it." Author Byron Katie in her book **Loving What Is** says, "To think that I know what's best for anyone else is to be out of *my* business. Even in the name of love, it is pure arrogance, and the result is tension, anxiety, and fear. Do I know what's right for me? That is my own business. Let me work with that before I try to solve problems for you."

Is there ever any time I should get involved with someone else's monkeys or circus? Maybe. That's something only we can individually decide. But I'll bet most of the time we do it unconsciously and out of habit without really thinking about whether it is something better left to the other person who "owns" it. And any time we are doing it with the underlying hope for approval, acceptance or love, chances are good that we are using it as a distraction (and excuse) from living our own life as fully and completely as possible. Maybe, just maybe, the SMART path would be for each of us to focus, learn from, and ultimately enjoy our own monkeys, and let everyone else do the same.

Chapter Twelve

Using Memories To Rewrite Our Past & Create Our Future

"What you think about, talk about, and do something about is what comes about. Your thoughts, words, and actions either move you closer to where you want or further away from where you want to be." ~Larry Winget

I am the second daughter of a family of four girls. If you asked any of us what we remember about our childhood and our parents, you would definitely receive four different answers. One is adamant that both my parents were alcoholics. Another one is convinced they were the best parents in the world. Who's right? Both actually. That's because the chosen memories each of us holds in our minds determines the story of our past. Unfortunately, even though you and I would like to believe our memories are flawless, they are seldom an accurate portrayal of what really happens at any given time. Instead, the majority of our memories are a process that we use to make meaning and sense of our experiences. But with most of that process unconscious, the quality of both our past and our future reflects the stories we habitually focus on and tell. Want a better future? Choose to remember, and then tell, a better story about your past.

Could it really be that simple? Well no. That's because the way we create our memories is a complicated business. Fortunately for all of us, science now proves that altering them in a positive way is possible. Reading up on some of the latest in memory research is a good place to start.

Generally, most of us think of our memory as a DVR or video recorder. We think that when something happens in our lives, our minds "record" the information and store it away until needed. Yet even though most of us admit we routinely forget large chunks of what happened, we still persist in thinking that it is possible to recall information and events accurately. While some of us are better at it than others, the vast majority of us do worse than we acknowledge.

What's going on? Basically, our memories all begin with our sensory perception. We like to believe we know and observe everything going on around us all the time, but we actually only perceive a tiny percentage of the input happening at any given moment. Of course, consciously and unconsciously we pre-guide our minds to primarily pay attention to things we believe are important, unique or threatening. The remaining thousands of bits of input are then lost in an instant.

Once we focus on and perceive something, we usually hold that perception in our short-term memory to evaluate whether we want to continue to "store" it or not. Sadly, our short-term memory is quite limited. On the average, most people can only hold seven things in their mind for approximately 20 to 30 seconds.

However, when something is important enough, and judged by us as worthy of remembering, the perception is transferred to our long-term memory banks for future use. Still, what we later recall isn't really the exact observation. Instead, what we store is the overall general idea of the memory—the "gist" of the story—based upon how we choose to interpret it. Even when we manage to hang on to a few of the more important details, what we really recollect is often inaccurate. As author and psychologist Leonard Mlodinow says in his book *Subliminal*, "…when pressed for the unremembered details, even well-intentioned people making a sincere effort to be accurate will inadvertently fill in the gaps by making things up." Unfortunately, that's a big problem because as Mlodinow continues, "People will believe the memories they make up."

That's where the memory problem becomes really tricky. Mlodinow mentions several studies that show when we repeatedly tell our interpretation of the story, and then recall it at a later date, "there wasn't just memory loss; there were also memory additions." With time we tend to "smooth out" our memories and fit them into a comfortable narration that fits our prior knowledge of the world. It is very human to want to find meaning and make sense of the world and our experiences. So, whenever we remember something, we are rewriting our memories into a story that fits our "prior knowledge and beliefs," and even our "preformed tendencies and bias." In fact, Mlodinow is convinced that with memory, "Inaccuracy was the rule, not the exception."

Quite a few humorous examples exist that show how mistaken we can be when we rely on our memory. Anyone remember the TV show **Candid Camera**? A phenomenon called, "change blindness" shows how we often mistakenly recall a person asking for direction when it happens in real world interactions. Regrettably, these false memories or stories frequently have tragic repercussions. **The Innocence Project**, an organization that uses DNA testing to exonerate those wrongfully convicted of crimes reports that 73% of those cases overturned through DNA testing were based on eyewitness testimony. In other words, the victims involved pinpointed the wrong person nearly 75% of the time. According to Mlodinow, police know without a doubt that about 20 to 25% of the time a witness will identify the wrong person in a line up simply because the police know that person was a "plant." With such routine inaccuracies, relying on eyewitness identification is extremely unreliable.

The implications of how our faulty memories affect our day-to-day lives are huge, but most of us remain unaware. Recent studies verify that false memories can be implanted by suggestion to subjects and can literally help shape new attitudes and preferences. Examples include what kinds of food to eat or avoid, alcohol consumption quantity and preferences, and even voting preferences and how we remember political events. Each of these show how memories are susceptible to being altered by changing what it is we think we remember. Photo doctoring is an especially powerful way to plant false memories—as is asking the "right leading question" at the right time. For the most part, the new memory is more accepted when congruent with prior attitudes and evaluations, but that they can be so easily altered is worthy of deep consideration. As an article about memory written in 2010 in **Slate Magazine** says, "The scary part is that your memories have already been altered. Much of what you recall about your life never happened, or it happened in a very different way."

The good news in all of this is that if our memories can be adjusted without us knowing about it, we can also work to alter them in a proactive and positive way to rewrite our past and then create a better future! In his book *Hardwiring Happiness,* Rick Hanson Ph.D. is convinced that with practice and focus we can effectively train our brains and "sensitize it toward the positive" on a regular basis. Using several techniques described in his book, he also says "taking in the good is the deliberate internalization of positive experience in implicit memory." So with intention and effort, it is possible to rewrite our experiences and memories in ways that bring us more peace, happiness and meaning.

Obviously the more difficult and traumatic the memory the more challenge we will face in changing them. But the work of people like Dr. Elizabeth Loftus, considered the premier memory doctor in the world, proves that completely unreal memories can be planted if we never question what it is we think we experienced—especially when the new "memory" comes from someone we trust. Yet in the end, at least according to **Slate Magazine**, Dr. Loftus believes the primary purpose of this innate ability is to "conveniently adjust" what we think we remember in order to "promote happiness or, at least, to avoid depression." So perhaps it's advisable to use it to heal and help, rather than perpetually endorse or reinforce a tragic past.

Each of my sisters and I have the choice, yes the CHOICE, to decide the quality of our past and our memories of our parents. After all, every person's life is usually filled with a collection of both good and bad experiences. What we individually choose to focus on, highlight, and repeatedly tell others, and ourselves, can either lead to a happier life, or reinforce the past negatively. Even when it's not easy, it is important to remember it is possible.

Obviously this short chapter cannot offer all the studies available that prove that our memory is largely a fictional story that we choose to believe. Still, it is also good to keep in mind that there are techniques that can help rewrite and alter those stories, and the book *Hardwiring Happiness* is one way to start. What is SMART and essential above all, is to acknowledge that we are the authors of the story of our lives and that the book is never ever, ever finished as long as we still walk the earth. Until then, let's keep rewriting the story until we achieve the happiness and peace we seek.

Chapter Thirteen

How Values & Rightsizing Are Clues To Enjoying The Journey Instead of The Destination

"…there is also a mechanism called a 'rudder'— that is, your thinking, your approach to triumphs and defeats, joys and pain and losses, the stuff no one escapes—that calibrates one's happiness. That rudder won't shelter you from a hurricane as you venture across the ocean, but it will absolutely color how much you enjoy the trip…your thinking is your experience." ~Barbara Bradley Hagerty

As many of you know, I've been writing about rightsizing for several years now. The concept of rightsizing constantly helps me to focus on designing a meaningful life journey—not a particular destination I'll ever fully experience. So when I recently came across an article about how values offer a similar perspective, it caught my interest.

I've now discovered that values, like rightsizing, are a direction. Sort of like getting in the car and heading north. We might be more north than we were yesterday, but we'll never actually *arrive*. Once we discover how to live our values or how to rightsize our life, we are better able to appreciate the road we are traveling, regardless of whether we hit a few road bumps or whether we ever even reach a final destination.

In many ways, values are the opposite of goals and demonstrate why so many of us have a difficult time reaching them. In most cases, goals are all about the outcome. Sometimes we reach them—sometimes not. Values, on the other hand, are not something you can own or even "find." We CHOOSE our values and allow them to direct our path. So goals are like a target we aim at, while values are the actual bow and arrows that we use to aim and motivate ourselves with along the way. Most of the time if we miss the target, we aren't happy. But if we master the art of archery, the very practice is a pleasure in itself.

Of course, goals are beneficial too. But far too often they remind us of what we don't have, rather than what we do. And if the end destination is our primary focus, then we never feel satisfied and are always striving for more. Values, on the other hand, give every step of the journey meaning and purpose. Like author and professor, Steven C. Hayes says, "Values get you to enough; they make this moment about something that you hold dear."

It is the same with my version of rightsizing. While many in the sustainable or minimalist view promote tactics and goals a person needs to reach to find fulfillment, I believe that the act of moving TOWARDS rightsizing is rewarding in every moment. I'll never live in a "tiny" house and instead strive to keep my current house as rightsized as possible.

I won't ever only own just 100 things (as is sometimes promoted) but the things I do own are important to me. I still work (I'm not retired) but the work I do fills each of my days with purpose and meaning. Rightsizing to me means stripping away those things that don't matter, and aiming towards those things that do, every single day.

Like I said above, Steven C. Hayes says much of the same about values. A foundation professor at the University of Nevada, he is the author of 44 books and nearly 600 scientific articles. His work is primarily focused "on the nature of human language and the cognition and application of this to the understanding and alleviation of human suffering." With his study of behavioral sciences, he has developed Acceptance and Commitment Therapy (ACT). It is from this study that he has begun to recognize the importance of values to aid in all of us becoming thriving individuals.

What does it matter? I believe the bottom line is that when we know the direction we choose our life to go, we can handle everything that lies ahead. In some ways, values are the tools we use to design what we feel gives our life meaning. What matters to me, what makes my life fulfilling, is likely different from yours. But once we know what ours are, we can use them to head in that direction regardless of what pops up along the way. Sure we have good days, hopefully lots of them. But even if things aren't going as planned, we still hold on to the meaning behind our direction.

Recent politics offer a great example. When I started writing this blog post it was before the election in the U.S. Hopes were very high in many ways—a good goal for sure. But now that the election is over, if all our hope was tied to one particular outcome or one particular candidate—we are either happy or sad. Instead, when we focus on our individual values, we can still feel that our efforts had meaning and we can feel fulfilled with the experience. Values like 1) connections with other like-minded people, 2) compassion for underprivileged people, 3) community involvement and 4) greater understanding about the world around me that allowed me to wake up feeling good this morning regardless of who did or didn't win.

So how do we know we are focused on the process (values) rather than the outcome (goals)? According to Hayes, there are several things to ask yourself?

#1 Do I have a sense of *enough*, rather than a need to measure whether the outcome was more or less than I hoped for or expected?

#2 Can I readily name my heroes and do they stand for the qualities I believe in most?

#3 Am I in touch with the sweetest and most rewarding moments of my life?

#4 Do I recognize where I am most vulnerable and why? Hayes believes that "we hurt where we care."

#5 Do I spend a lot of time just entertaining myself or dulling the pain of my life instead of striving towards what matters to me?

#6 What would I do, what do I do, even if no one notices or knows whether I was the one who did it?

#7 What is it that makes me get up in the morning?

#8 If I only had ten minutes to write about something that really matters to me, what would I write about?

#9 Do I care more about what other people care about, or more about what really matters to me?

#10 Are having things (like a big house, a new car, lots of money in the bank) more important to me than what I can do with my mind, time, money and energy?

In retrospect, it is easy to see how each of these questions asks us to focus on what really matters to us. Obviously, that is a key to values as well as rightsizing. But according to Hayes, it isn't just a matter of determining what matters to us, it is then consciously choosing to make those values our lifetime roadmap as we travel through life. Yet, as Hayes points out, today's world is very good at distracting us into blindly following the herd in just about every area of life. If we were raised to believe that happiness only comes by graduating from college, getting a high paying job, buying a big house, having 2.5 kids and a big screen tv, then it takes conscious awareness to pull back and decide that living our values are more important. As with rightsizing, the temptation to want more, more, more of anything, at any cost, is high.

It doesn't take a giant leap of understanding to recognize why so many people in today's world are bewildered and without hope. Hayes makes a powerful argument that without a clear understanding of our values we are rudderless in a vast ocean of information supplied by technology and the marketing industry. Like standing open-mouthed before a fire hose, we can literally drown in the flood of toxic information being directed at us. It is difficult enough as adults, can we imagine the bewilderment of our children today?

Hayes believes that all humans strive toward connection, compassion, and communication, but it takes the right values to guide us in those directions. Like rightsizing, determining our values helps us to focus in on what really gives our lives meaning and purpose. They also help us get through the tough times. Like Friedrich Nietzsche said, "He who has a strong enough WHY can bear almost any HOW."

Values and rightsizing keep us on course no matter what is happening in the world or our individual lives. As Hayes says, "There are many ways to walk a valued journey." The SMART perspective is to use the best nudges to keep our life on course.

Chapter Fourteen

Mindfulness—The Cure For A Busy & Overthinking Mind

> *"We are what we think. All that we are*
> *arises with our thoughts. With our thoughts,*
> *we make our world." ~The Buddha*

Who are you? I mean who are you, really? I think it is easy for all of us to forget sometimes that we are more than the skin-encapsulated egos that we wake up as every morning. Even when we stop and pause to remember that we are more than our minds and egos, it's far too easy to fall asleep and slip into our frequently unconscious way of living. That's why the practice of mindfulness holds such promise. In fact, reading the new book *The Mindfulness Edge* by Matt Tenny and Tim Gard, Ph.D., helped me go beyond merely understanding why heightened awareness is so beneficial, to a deeper edge of the practice itself.

In case you are wondering, I have meditated on and off

for nearly twenty years, and now consistently every single day for over ten. I've read dozens of books and hundreds of articles about meditation and mindfulness, so the idea isn't new to me. I'm well aware of the many benefits that meditation offers and the research into how valuable mindfulness can be for all sorts of situations and conditions. So when offered the book for review, I was a bit skeptical. Would it really offer me anything new? The good news is yes.

What is Mindfulness?

In case some of you are new to the concept, mindfulness is simple and slightly different from the practice of meditation. Some of it connects, but there is a difference. Tenny describes the action of being mindful as, "Being nonjudgmentally aware of what is being experienced—including thoughts and emotions—in the present moment." It is an awareness that includes self-awareness. The thing is, we don't just decide to be aware. Mindful self-awareness is a skill needing development.

Unfortunately, most of the time, most of us go around living life governed by our thinking minds and our egos. Some neuroscientists call that unconscious perspective the default mode network (DMN). The DMN filters all of our perceptions based on past experiences, our reoccurring habits, and any beliefs or opinions we have formed throughout our lives—regardless of whether it's true or not. The problem is, unless we are mindfully aware, we can't tell the difference between the truth and a huge error in our minds.

Making matters worse, according to the book, 47% of the time our minds are wandering or daydreaming rather than being focused on what is in front of us. Even if we manage to grasp some awareness now and then, we don't usually hold on to it very long. As Tenny says, "We spend most of our time being that voice inside our heads that is constantly analyzing, judging or just blabbering about nonsense, and which is often accompanied by mental images that capture more of our attention than the outside world."

Think you are better than most? Tenny offers this, "People who think they are completely free from habitual, conditioned ways of thinking, deciding and acting are often those who are the least free from their programming. The more unaware we are of our conditioning, the more unconscious we become."

Why is mindfulness so beneficial?

#1 It helps us make better choices and decisions for others and ourselves.

One of the biggest problems with habitual DMN thinking is that it limits our choices and decisions. Rather than considering whether something is genuinely good or bad for us, we just act on whatever comes by default. Then the more ingrained the habit becomes, the more we do it again and again without making clear or conscious choices based upon our own best interests. Tenny cites studies in his book where just two weeks of mindfulness training reduced mind wandering and helped with focus. Even better, it allows people to keep their thinking creative, agile, and to make clearer choices regarding money and resources.

In addition, mindfulness training allows our brains to work more efficiently. Studies done using brain scans from mindfulness practitioners show that they experience more efficient executive control. Practitioners also displayed better mental performance when given tests after mindfulness training. An added benefit by Dr. Gard is, "…findings suggest that mindfulness can reduce normal age-related decline in fluid intelligence and integration of functional brain networks."

#2 It provides a space where we are free from conditioning.

Ever get your buttons pushed? Regrettably most of us go through life reacting to what we see on the news, who said what to whom, and what's going on moment by moment. Mindfulness gives us both the awareness and space to actually choose how to respond rather than operating out of habit or unconsciousness behavior. As author and neurologist Viktor Frankl said, "Between stimulus and response there is a space. In that space lies our freedom and power to choose our response. In our response lies our growth and freedom."

#3 It allows us to be more emotionally intelligent.

Ever been in a situation when you got angry and then later regretted it? Ever started to cry and really wished you didn't? Do you startle easily? Studies show that people trained in mindfulness have greater emotional control than the general population. Other research done by the U.S. Military highlights how such training can help reduce stress, chronic pain and even help people recover faster from things like PTSD.

In addition, this type of awareness practice helps people become more familiar and comfortable with change, less dependent on what others think of them, and more resilient in the face of any unpleasant emotions. Again, mindfulness creates space around our emotions allowing us to process them in a way that is beneficial rather than automatic.

Mindfulness training not only helps us to be more emotionally mature, it also increases empathy, compassion and altruism. Research shows that only eight weeks of training is enough to increase our ability to empathize with other people significantly, and to take compassionate action.

What does it take to be more mindful?

Practice, practice and more practice. Sorry, there is no pill or simple action to achieve the desired result although the book does offer simple steps to take. What is essential is the need to "stabilize awareness" and that requires ongoing practice. Tenny suggests over and over that, "we are training to be aware of our thinking, instead of being pulled into becoming our thinking."

This is where meditation can help. Although there are many ways to meditate, the practice of sitting and watching our thoughts in the here and now without judgment or comparison is a good place to start. Sounds simple, right? The problem is that most of the time we aren't living in the present time, we are worrying about something that's going to happen or fussing about something that happened in the past. Our thoughts run around like a wild monkey in our brain. Again, mindfulness allows us to put "space" around our thoughts so that we can let go of comparison, judgment and control of the outcome. Want to let go of your busy and overthinking mind? Create the space, breathe, and let it go.

It's difficult to say what particular suggestions in this book made the biggest impression on me, but I do know that my appreciation of mindfulness has deepened from where it was before. Of particular interest is the idea of the "space" around my thoughts and emotions. The book also reminds us of our interconnection with everyone and everything. Again, though not a new idea, it reminded me that each one of us is so much more than just our thinking or our egos. I'm not certain whether this book can help others know who they are on the deepest level. But I'm positive that the practice of mindfulness can point us in the right direction. And asking and attempting to answer those questions with awareness is a very SMART thing to do.

Chapter Fifteen

Are You A Ruminator Or An Anticipator?

"I am determined to be cheerful and happy
in whatever situation I may find myself. For
I have learned that the greater part of our
misery or unhappiness is determined not by
our circumstance but by our
disposition." ~Martha Washington

It recently occurred to me that people are generally of
two types—anticipators or ruminators. Sure, most of the
attention goes to whether or not people are positive or
negative. But I've witnessed some people who claim to be
optimists, and yet they overthink and obsess about their past,
their worries or their claims of injustice nearly every day.
Perhaps it is SMART to consider other possible directions for
our focus and explore ways to calibrate our attention in a more
helpful way.

First, let me define the differences by way of an
example. My husband Thom and I are fortunate to work with a

married couple in their nineties. And when I say work, I do mean work. Larry first contracted with Thom over 25 years ago when Larry was just an alert youngster of 68. From the beginning, Thom admitted that Larry was exceptionally forward thinking. Later we met his wife Joanne and realized they both possess the ability to leave behind and let go of details from the past. At the same time, they almost immediately shift their attention to what is on the horizon.

During the last 25 years, with Thom's help, Larry and Joanne have successfully bought, owned and sold dozens of commercial properties. Most of the time, they make money, but not always. It doesn't seem to affect them much either way. If it works out well—they are glad for a minute. If it crumbles and falls—they are grumpy for a minute. Either way, their conversation quickly shifts to the next deal, the next event, the next happening. Sure, at their age they've had some health challenges, but you'll never hear them complain or ramble about specifics. I consider them "poster children" for positive anticipation. It's certainly no wonder that at 93 and 92 respectively, every conversation they have is a focus on all the positive things that are happening now and in the future.

At the same time, I know another couple named Bill and Carol. Both Bill and Carol are 30 years younger than Larry and Joanne. They work hard and have risen to some degree of success in their lives. But if you sit and talk with them for any length of time the conversation always drifts to things that happened that keep them from enjoying life today. Their focus seems to obsess over what has gone wrong, what should be different, and things that can never be figured out. And like the Bruce Springsteen song "Glory Days," they regularly talk about the good old days when they were young, carefree, and their future looked bright. I consider them stuck in rumination.

Of course, if you study the psychological aspects of rumination, you'll find that it is much more involved than living in the past. In many cases, it is a sign of deep depression and constantly obsessing or overthinking about things that simply cannot be changed or understood. Women tend to ruminate more than men, perhaps because we make relationships a priority and those are often fraught with uncertainty. Unfortunately, rumination is usually a vicious cycle that gets worse if not kept in check.

The Negative Consequences of Rumination

According to researchers, the habitual cycle of rumination often:

- Hinders thinking and problem-solving;

- Pushes away people who can provide social support and friendship;

- Promotes addictions and other unhealthy behaviors;

- Destroys confidence and keeps one from taking steps

to alleviate the problem;

- Triggers depression (up to four times as often) and keeps a person depressed;

Is Rumination Just Another Name For Worry?

According to a study done by Susan Nolen-Hoeksema, Blair Wisco, and Sonja Lyubomirsky, the primary reason people worry or ruminate is to control or deal with uncertainty. However, those researchers believe that there is a significant difference between the two strategies. Here is clarification.

Worry is usually:

1. Future-oriented;

2. Focused on anticipated threat;

3. Contains the CONSCIOUS motive to anticipate and prepare for threat;

4. Contains the UNCONSCIOUS motivation to avoid core negative outcomes and painful images;

On the other hand, **rumination** is usually:

1. More past/present oriented;

2. Focused on issues of self-worth, meaning, themes of loss, making sense of what's happened;

3. Contains the CONSCIOUS motive to understand the deeper meaning of events, gain insight and solve problems;

4. Contains the UNCONSCIOUS motivation to avoid troubling situations, making changes or responsibility for taking action;

The differences are further explained by Nolen-Hoeksema, et al., who said, "…when people are worrying, they are uncertain about their ability to control important outcomes, but they have some belief that they could control those outcomes if they just try (or worry) hard enough. In contrast, when people are ruminating, they are more certain that important outcomes are definitely uncontrollable."

Of course, an individual who is worrying or ruminating can shift back and forth between the two states depending upon the circumstances. But usually, when a person sees the situation as hopeless and beyond their ability to control, they are ruminating. And as stated above, the negative consequences of rumination can then grow until the ruminator feels completely devastated and can do nothing positive to get off of the hamster-wheel they have built for themselves.

How To Let Go Of Thoughts That Bind You

The good news is that unless a person's rumination has escalated into severe depression, there are things they can do to make the situation better. One of the easiest ways to stop ruminating is to distract yourself when you find yourself obsessing or overthinking any problem, situation or relationship. In other words, let go of the idea that you can ever figure it out or get to the hidden meaning.

According to the study done by Susan Nolen-Hoeksema and others, diverting our attention to something that is "absorbing, engaging and capable of providing positive reinforcement," can lift our mood and relieve our depressive symptoms." That distraction can be as simple as, "going for a run or a bike ride, seeing a movie with friends, or concentrating on a project at work."

Of course, those who routinely ruminate often find it easier to use negative distractors (like imagining something disastrous for example) instead of looking for thoughts that are more positive. Like any habit, if the mind is conditioned to look for the negative, it is much harder to see anything BUT the negative. And because that negative bias exists within them, they more easily are led to destructive behaviors (like addictions) to reduce the pain.

Bottom Line

It's easy just to tell someone to "think positive

thoughts." But what this information about rumination tells me is that if you are a ruminator at heart, it's a lot harder to distract yourself in a positive way. So, what's a person to do? As the researchers quoted earlier suggest, we must find something that engages us personally.

Also beneficial is looking honestly at our high expectations for ourselves, others and even the events we judge. Much of what causes an escalation of rumination is seeking unattainable goals, perfectionism or tying up our self-esteem in one area of our life. Instead, learning to take small steps towards goals that give us a sense of having control (however small), can lead to improvement.

Positive self-reflection is also helpful. But again, if a person is prone to rumination they might just reflect repeatedly on beating themselves up and feeling hopeless. The key to making it positive is asking, "Do I call my self-reflection 'brooding' or do I call it 'pondering'?" If we can make that distinction, we may discover the more helpful aspects of the experience.

It's also important to note that a key to moving beyond rumination is learning to problem-solve and reflect in a positive way. Remember, rumination is often about avoiding actions we don't want to take, and what that change might mean in our lives. That's why another valuable strategy is to practice mindfulness or meditation. Again, this is not to let the mind spin out of control in negativity, but instead to learn to train the mind in a more beneficial direction. Or like Nolen-Hoeksema and others say, "The key to therapy is for people to stop automatically accepting the true value of their negative thoughts and to choose to substitute these thoughts with more rational or adaptive ones." They also remind us that we always have the ability to change things—even if it is just changing our minds about what's happening.

Naturally, this article cannot explore all of the subtleties of rumination but what it looks like and how it feels is something I think many of us can relate to even if only occasionally. Do we spend our time anticipating positive things for the future, or ruminate and brood over things we can't change or even know for certain? As always the SMART approach is to do our best to stay as awake, aware and mindful in the moment as possible—and then decide. So, which are you?

Chapter Sixteen

The Five Most Helpful Messages I Get From Abraham-Hicks

*"Sometimes you can change your conditions.
Always you can change your
mind." ~Abraham-Hicks*

It's no secret that I am a fan of Abraham-Hicks. I've written about her/them before and shared different thoughts that they generate in me on a regular basis. But every now and then someone will ask me why I continue to listen to them over and over. That's when it occurred to me that I have never shared some of the overriding themes that I most appreciate and what keeps me coming back for more. What I think it boils down to are the following five messages that are woven into every lecture—and why I believe that these messages offer both encouragement and support for us all.

The source of Abraham-Hicks is a woman named Esther Hicks. Hicks, along with her late husband Jerry, began what she calls "tapping into Infinite Intelligence" back in the mid-1980s. Hicks calls the messages she receives "the teachings of Abraham." And regardless of whether the true source of this inspiration comes from Hick's own mind or something beyond, most of the material is uplifting and helpful to millions of people around the world—including me. Do I accept it all? Absolutely not. But then again, there is no author/speaker/teacher that I accept 100%. But that doesn't stop me from keeping my mind open to any message that adds practical benefits to my life.

With that in mind, here are five reoccurring themes from Abraham-Hicks that I find most helpful. (For clarification, I refer to Abraham-Hicks as "they/their/them.")

#1 Unconditional love and acceptance. The number one reason I continue to listen to their message is for the ongoing words of unconditional love and acceptance. And trust me—I have been studying positive, uplifting and spiritual messages for most of my life. My explorations have touched on all the world's major religions, lots of new age ones, many of the popular philosophers, pop-psychologists, writers and dozens of motivational speakers. While many of those resources offer inspiring messages and encourage us to love each other as we love ourselves—none top Abraham-Hicks in my humble opinion.

Why? The best way to explain it might be from my first impression of their work. When I first heard about them and read a bit of their first book I wasn't impressed. At first glance the message seems extremely materialistic and self-centered. Whoever thought THAT was a good idea? If you've ever read and/or watched the movie **The Secret** (with its message of Law of Attraction and often promoted by Abraham-Hicks) it makes the Universe sound like a slot machine that pays off if you follow the right directions. In other words, once you figure out the "law" it is all about getting, getting, getting.

Then for some reason years later I happened across one of their lectures on the internet and listened. Then I found another and listened again. And behind the message of Law of Attraction I began hearing that it was more about "The Universe" saying yes and affirming whatever we choose– UNCONDITIONALLY, rather than just about getting.

Now if I haven't lost you completely, and I hope I haven't, then let me explain what I've learned through the years. Sure, a lot of people are drawn to them and Law of Attraction (LOA) because it seems like a formula for getting "stuff." Stuff might be money, relationships, better jobs or just a big fancy house. The thing is, Abraham-Hicks doesn't care. Abraham-Hicks never judges and says, oh, you can't have that. They never suggest that wanting isn't spiritual, nice or what a good person should even think of asking for. Instead, Abraham-Hicks teaches that the Universe responds to our thoughts and desires with a big "Yes!" That pure message of love is about as close to witnessing a mother's unconditional acceptance that I have ever imagined. Sure, lots of people use it strictly to get more stuff and that sounds incredibly greedy. But that is mostly entry-level LOA. And you know what? If you keep listening to Abraham-Hicks you will find that the message goes far beyond that—and if you have the ability and desire to go further—you find that it isn't about getting all that stuff at all. Instead, it leads to the second theme that I appreciate.

#2 No matter what it is that we think we want or desire, what we really want is THE FEELING(s) we think it will bring— not the thing itself. Whoa! If you were thinking that LOA or Abraham-Hicks was materialistic and selfish, this one might cause you to pause a bit. I don't think the message hit me hard until I had listened to dozens of their lectures. Slowly I began to realize that true unconditional love and acceptance doesn't judge us in any way—including our materialistic wants and desires. It loves us regardless.

If you are anything like me and raised in a Christian Religion you know that even though the message there is one of unconditional love and acceptance—it always seems to come with a very high level of conditions and rules. I also found traces of those conditions and expectations in other religions and philosophies I studied. Not so with Abraham-Hicks. You are loved. You are accepted. There are no rules except we reap what we sow. What we send out, we get back. It is done unto us what we believe. We are not punished FOR our beliefs, but by our beliefs.

But lest you think that such a message leads to us all

acting in selfish and hurtful ways to others and ourselves, that leads me to the third of their basic themes.

#3 All our suffering comes from our sloppy or erroneous thinking. Abraham-Hicks isn't the first to bring up this fundamental truth. For thousands of years the teachings of Buddha and other ancient religions have been sharing that if we can get our thinking in alignment with the fundamental nature of the universe then we can eliminate the pain and suffering that we experience. Of course, how we get rid of that erroneous thinking usually differs from teacher to teacher, but the message stays the same. If we continue to hang on to certain thoughts, emotions and their corresponding actions, then we will either experience peace and the rewards of that, or the direct opposite.

That then leads to the fourth message I find most valuable.

 # 4 We came to create reality, not accept it. Now I get that on the surface that sounds a bit crazy. Surely, you and I can't change reality? The thing is, Abraham-Hicks teaches that the only reality that exists for me is "mine." And the same goes for you. Obviously, I can't change the is-ness of present conditions, and I certainly can't change anyone else, but I can control my own mental perceptions. And the level at which I am able to do that, the more I create my own individual reality and corresponding future. I certainly can't stop a bullet with my bare hands or jump off a mountain without facing the law of gravity in a dire way, but again, how I view and interpret ANY EXPERIENCE in my life is my creation.

Of course, it isn't just about interpretation either. I either participate and design my life in ways that I intend, or I let the people around me and their interpretations tell me what I should and should not do. If I trust that the source of creation flows through me, not some other anointed being telling me how it should be, then I co-create my reality. I am not the source of it, I am only allowing it to work through me. This message is incredibly liberating if you give yourself permission to follow it down the rabbit hole. And finally, this leads to the fifth message of value.

#5 Our ultimate intention while here on Earth is alignment with our Source (no matter what we call Source). Like I mentioned earlier, my first impression of Abraham-Hicks was that it was all about me-me-me. Yet, the more I listened the more I kept hearing the broader perspective of what they teach. They point out that the vast majority of us are raised believing everyone in authority knows what is best for us, and if we don't comply, then we are bad, sinful or at least wrong. That pressure is there if we don't do everything our parents tell us, regardless of how wise our parents really are. Those same messages lie in our school system, many religious systems, our peers and certainly our culture. Over and over and over we are taught that we must play by the rules and commandments set up by other people and institutions if we want to be loved, have friends, be successful and/or even to go to heaven.

Abraham-Hicks says no. We came for our own alignment and when we find that deep connection you might think that would lead to anarchy on every level—again the message is no. In fact, Abraham-Hicks teaches that the most horrendous actions by anyone come from those who are cut off and disconnected from their Source. Once connected and aligned, no one would ever cause harm or hurt to any other living being.

I get that there are lots of messages in the world today that may or may not be helpful. But I can honestly say that since I began listening to Abraham-Hicks I have found a deeper peace about who I truly am. And I can't help but believe the more accepting of myself I am, then the more accepting I am of others. I've become far less likely to think anyone else controls my happiness and wellbeing, and far more likely to look within. I have also developed a much deeper relationship with my inner being and am far more in touch with my feelings.

Regardless of where the teachings of Abraham-Hicks originate, they have made a positive difference in my life. As always, the SMART approach is to keep an open mind, find what works well for us and then do our best to live those ideas 365.

Chapter Seventeen

Lessons From A Magic Shop For A Happy & Healthy Life

"You are going to go through life either by design or by default" ~ *Rick Warren*

Wouldn't it be nice to walk into a store and be handed an instruction manual for living a happy and healthy life? A man named James Doty was offered exactly that back when he was twelve years old. This last week while I was researching another topic, I stumbled upon a podcast by James Doty and immediately knew that his story had the potential to change lives. Of course, even when we have a map right in front of us, that doesn't mean that we always take the right turns at the right time or the path is without peril. Still, Doty's story offers us all a glimpse of things we can each do to create the life we feel called to live.

So, who is James Doty and what makes his story worth telling? Doty, MD, is a clinical professor of Neurosurgery at Stanford University and the director of the Center for

Compassion and Altruism Research at Stanford University School of Medicine. While his current credentials are quite impressive, he started with extremely humble beginnings. Living below the poverty level, with a father who was an alcoholic and a mother who was an invalid, he was well on his way to becoming a juvenile delinquent. By his own admission, he felt hopeless like a leaf being tossed around in the wind. No control. No future.

One day he found himself wandering the streets of Lancaster, CA. In a lone strip-mall, he saw a magic shop and went inside. There he met a grandmotherly woman named Ruth who was filling in for her son who owned the shop. When Doty asked her how magic worked, Ruth explained that it worked because most people aren't that aware to begin with. She told him that although our brains are very busy, they are also extremely lazy, and easily distracted. But rather than being distracted by hand gestures, most of the time people aren't even watching the magic in the first place. Instead, they are regretting something they did yesterday or worrying about something that is supposed to happen tomorrow. Magic works because it is easy to trick people who aren't paying attention.

After talking for about 20 minutes, Ruth told Doty that she would be available for the next six weeks and if Doty returned every day to talk to her, she would teach him real magic. Doty admits he had no great illusions of grandeur—he simply had nothing else better to do. So, for the following six weeks he came to the store every single day and Ruth taught him the magic that changed his life.

In case you are wondering, the whole and complete story about what Doty learns and where it leads him is explained in his book, **Into the Magic Shop**. I did not read the book although I am definitely tempted because of the powerful reviews. What I did learn was available by doing some research and I think the points made are a wonderful introduction into the so-called-magic that Ruth taught that so fully transformed his experience.

Relax the body

Sounds simple right? Yet, even those of us who know the benefits of such a practice often convince ourselves that we don't have the time. Basically, Ruth first taught young Doty a few simple techniques that helped him focus his attention on his body, to become more mindful in the present moment and to relax—all important for an impulsive and reactive young man.

Tame the mind

Once the body is relaxed, the next lesson is to focus on quieting the mind and bringing it in to focus. The primary technique Ruth taught young Doty was meditation. By meditating on either the breath, a candle flame or a simple mantra, Ruth explained that Doty would be able to eventually calm his thoughts and concentrate on ideas and sensations that were helpful and uplifting. Of course, Ruth also explained that this takes time and should be done every day for 20-30 minutes. Plus, it isn't something you do a couple of times and have it perfected. It can easily take weeks (or much longer) before any significant changes occur. However, the more you practice it, the more you will be able to simply observe without attachment any thoughts that are negative or distracting. You should also be able to disengage from any emotional reactions that are not helpful. Eventually, this ongoing practice keeps your mind at peace while also holding your body in a state of relaxation and wellbeing.

Clarify your intent

After you have relaxed the body and fully focused the mind, the next step is to visualize those goals or experiences you wish to be or accomplish. Once your vision is clear, imagine as much detail around the goal as possible. See yourself having acquired the goal, or see it after the experience is over. What does that feel like? Where are you and who is with you? The more clarity you can provide the better. Repeating this activity once or twice every single day will help the vision become clearer and more detailed. Eventually, you will find yourself living the life you have imagined.

Doty does reveal that the pathway to what you say you want is seldom a straight line. At times it might seem that what you want is impossible to achieve, but similar to much of what Abraham-Hicks and LOA (Law of Attraction) teach, if you trust the process and stick with your vision it will eventually unfold.

So how did these life lessons work for James Doty? Spectacularly. After six weeks with Ruth, Doty believes his brain gradually rewired itself—reinforcing the idea of neural plasticity. He truthfully admitted that even though his outward circumstances didn't change—*he changed* and that made all the difference. Gradually he was able to stop responding to the negative dialogue running through his head. Eventually, instead of believing he was stuck without potential, he started believing he had unlimited potential. Not only did he finish high school, he went on to college and eventually became a very successful and wealthy neurosurgeon and businessman.

Unfortunately, at the pinnacle of his so-called success, he realized that he wasn't that happy or fulfilled. Even though his goals had manifested in every way possible, he realized that money and success were only reactions to that poverty-stricken young boy he used to be. Only after losing nearly all his wealth, status and many of his relationships, did he finally remember the other lesson that Ruth had taught him years ago.

Open your heart

Years earlier in that magic shop, Ruth had explained

that the greatest of the four lessons was the ability to open his heart. Regrettably, Doty missed most of that when he was young. A big aspect of that heart opening was to realize that we are all connected, and it is only through that connection and heartfelt awareness that we ever arrive at a place of peace and wellbeing. When we see others as ourselves and do what we can out of a compassionate heart, we will find the peace and happiness we desire. Having all the success and money in the world matters very little if our heart is closed and we are unconnected with the people we love.

So yes, all of these lessons are available for any of us to use beginning right now. Certainly, all of these ideas have been promoted and taught by writers, teachers, and sages throughout the centuries—so they aren't magic at all. But as with most magic, many of us aren't paying attention anyway. As Ruth said in the beginning, people are usually too busy worrying about what's to come or regretting what we did or didn't do in the past, so that we never take the time to believe in ourselves and be here now.

And let's also admit that most of us are too busy running around trying to make things happen in the world around us—instead of taking the time each day to shift our consciousness and *allow* things to change. I realize that relaxing our body, focusing our mind, visualizing and creating with an open heart aren't rocket science. But what each of them certainly offers are SMART ways to design a life that we say we want. It's true that some of us start with more advantages than others, but ultimately we always have the ability to respond in ways that serve us and lead to greater possibilities.

The good news is that the story doesn't just stop there. James Doty went on to use the same techniques to then re-create a life for himself that teaches the magic he learned to anyone who wants to listen. At the very center of his teaching now is the idea that compassion, and its companion kindness, are the most powerful magic of all. In fact, Doty admits that the greatest gift Ruth gave him was her time and attention. He is now convinced that we are wired to connect and care for one another and that the only way we will ever find the happiness and health we strive for is when we practice loving compassion with others and ourselves every single day. And never forget that is it SMART to practice that "magic" daily.

Chapter Eighteen

Don't Believe Your Shitty First Draft

"If you're going to live your life based on delusions (and you are, because we all do), then why not at least select a delusion that is helpful?" ~Elizabeth Gilbert

Ever had someone say something to you that felt like a punch in your gut? Even worse, ever have someone you care about do something that felt like a sharp knife in your heart? Fortunately, as I've gotten older, my extreme reactions are now further and further apart. But I'd be lying if I didn't admit that every now and then I still react in ways that are viscerally painful. Then this last week I was listening to a podcast interview of author Brene Brown and she shared something I found brilliant—as well as a perfect exercise to counteract those painful moments that catch us by surprise. And that practice is to remind myself *not* to believe my "shitty first draft."

As Brown explains, we all tell ourselves stories all the

time. I doubt I have to explain this to anyone who is a writer or who has been reading my blog (*SMART Living 365*) for any length of time. If we are aware stories are constantly being formed in our minds, we have the choice to do it in ways that either support us and inspire us—or tear us down and scare us to death. Now with Brown's help I have a new perspective that I had not considered before. It starts with her experience and research showing that whenever we feel threatened by anxiety, fear or loss, or whenever our shame is triggered in any way, our brains immediately and automatically demand a story about the situation to help us understand it.

The problem is, the fearful primitive part of our brain doesn't want a story with nuance or uncertainty. According to Brown, our brains usually default to a simple binary answer to the either/or questions of: Danger or safe? Good or bad? Helpful or hurtful? And also according to Brown, our stories usually exaggerate our greatest fears, shame triggers, and insecurities. So even if we remember we are telling ourselves stories about what is happening in the moment, unless we are really conscious, we can be startled into a reactionary state and immediately come up with a story that is filled with fear, anger and pain. Let me give you an embarrassing but true example.

Recently, Thom and I got together for dinner with friends. We laughed and talked about our plans for the coming summer and had an altogether great time. Or so I thought. A few days later Thom sent a text asking them about one of the plans they had mentioned that we were curious about. No answer. The next day I sent another text. Still no answer. Then, during my morning walk I walked by their house and saw a for sale sign in the yard!

For no other reason than I hadn't slept well the night before, my brain switched into reactionary mode and I immediately came up with a story that had me convinced that something horrible had been said during dinner and that they were moving out of state without telling us and no longer accepting our phone calls. Remember, the brain isn't looking for nuance or logic. It simply reacts to input in the most exaggerated way. And I probably don't need to tell you I have a very dramatic and creative mind that can easily build a mountain out of a molehill.

Fortunately, I had just listened to the podcast interview of Brene Brown and almost as quickly as I had come up with my dramatic rejection story, I told myself, "Well that's a really shitty first draft." And it's true. Not only was my first draft about as negative as it could be, it wasn't even close to true. But in a moment when we are feeling vulnerable, fearful or uncertain, we can easily convince ourselves that "danger" is everywhere. That's why remembering that I was only just telling myself a story about what I "thought" might be true, was the best thing I could do for myself. Of course this is just a minor example, but I'll bet you get the idea.

Brown then suggests that if we catch ourselves telling a shitty first draft that we ask ourselves, "How can I do a reality check on it?" In other words, if we can take the time to think it through logically and find out what is really happening, we will often discover that our first reaction wasn't *anywhere* near the truth. That's what happened to me when I took the time to talk to our friends and hear their side of *my* drama.

The problem is, if we keep running that shitty first draft through our minds over and over again, we can (okay I can!) easily come up with a 10-episode mini-series before I'm done! I think a lot of us can. Brown tells the story of how her son was convinced he was the dumbest kid in his class because he got a very low mark on a test. Only after Brown fact-checked the test with his teacher did he realize that the test was a new one and nearly everyone in the class did horribly too. Or what about the stories you might create when looking at all your friends having a fabulous life on Facebook?

Brown also explained how it is so easy to jump to (negative) conclusions with just about anything if we aren't careful. Again, the trick is to catch ourselves as quickly as possibly whenever we hear that shitty first draft going on in our heads and start on a more positive rewrite. Particularly problematic are close relationships, especially if we are feeling vulnerable. And it is almost always worse when our defenses are down and we aren't feeling healthy, strong or peaceful.

A key is to stop and pay attention to the story we are telling ourselves in any given situation. And make no mistake, we are telling ourselves stories all day long. The question is: is that story a shitty first draft that hasn't been fact-checked or edited? Or are we telling a well-researched story that accepts compassion, logic and nuance? I also believe that even if all the facts aren't going in our favor, we still have the ability to do multiple rewrites of any story so that it heads in a more healthy, compassionate and positive direction.

I don't know if I'll ever be able to turn off the storyteller in my mind. Sometimes she can amuse me, inspire me and comfort me just when I need it most. But if I don't pause and consider whether my first draft is worthy of the life I want to live, then it's time for a rewrite. The SMART thing to do is to remember that sometimes the story in our head is nothing more than a shitty first draft.

Chapter Nineteen

Choose To Remember That Everything Is Workable

"Hopelessness and happiness are both self-fulfilling prophecies. We become who we believe we can be." ~Mary Pipher

One of my favorite parables is the story of the light wolf and the dark wolf. Most of us know the light wolf as those parts in the world and in ourselves that are kind, loving, peaceful and hopeful. At the same time, the dark wolf represents all that is angry, fearful, greedy or hateful. Which one is most prominent in our lives? Simply—the one we feed. In other words, whichever wolf we focus on the most, nourishing it with our attention, time, words and Facebook posts, that's the one that grows and multiplies. The good news is of course that even if we realize we've been feeding the wrong wolf for far too long, it's never too late to make our light wolf strong, healthy and the biggest part of our lives.

This parable came to my mind after finishing a new book by Mary Pipher called, **Women Rowing North— Navigating Life's Currents & Flourishing As We Age.** Some of us may remember Pipher as the author of ***Reviving Ophelia.*** That book, written back in the 1990s, shared thoughts on the importance and necessity of nurturing teenage women through that tumultuous life-phase. Now hitting 70, Pipher understands that women in their third phase of life are also in an extremely transitional stage. The book is filled with her reflections, experience and advice from her own life history and those she has met and learned from along the way. I actually requested a review copy of this book instead of having a publicist solicit me, because I knew that it would contain nuggets that I can use to continue to create a happy and meaningful life. It does not disappoint.

But make no mistake, this is not a book that suggests that we all just need to think positively, and everything will be great. Some of the examples she uses throughout the book are of women who must face extremely difficult challenges with their own health or the health of their significant others or children. Some struggle with loneliness, finances, insurance, housing and any one of a number of life-trials that can peak as the years add up. Still, behind it all is a message of hope, possibility and the awareness that we do have the ability within to continue to feed that light wolf for as long as we live. Plus, it doesn't hurt to know that she confirms that research shows that women from the age of 65 to 79 are happiest of any demographic.

Pipher writes in a narrative that is both easy to read and inspirational. Throughout the book she sprinkles in ideas that had me reaching for my pen and underlining passages. With that in mind, here are a handful of those I want to remember.

- "As we age, we tend to improve our gratitude skills. Through trial and error learning, we know that if we focus on the good and positive, we see ourselves as lucky. Whereas, if we focus on grievances, past pains, regrets and disappointments, we make ourselves feel unlucky and miserable."

- "…happiness depends on how we deal with what we are given. Even though we all suffer, we don't all grow. Not all older women become elders…We don't become our wisest selves without effort."

- "We don't see the world as it is, but rather as we are. If we are angry and bitter, we find proof of hostility wherever we look. If we are trusting, we look for evidence of kindness. Growth requires us to constantly expand our point of view."

- "Not everyone experiences bliss as they age, but it is never too late to look for it. And if we look for it, we will find it…. Bliss doesn't happen because we are perfect or problem-free but rather because over the years we have become wise enough to be occasionally present for the moment. We have acquired the capacity to appreciate what simply is."

- "If we don't grow bigger, we can become bitter."

- "Attitude is not everything, but it is almost everything. In fact, in many situations it is all we have. Especially as we age, we can see clearly that we do not always have control, but we do have choices. That is our power."

- "There is always the possibility of self-rescue. We can choose where to focus our attention and will our way to gratitude."

- "The more we understand ourselves, the more skilled we will be at distinguishing between acting on impulse and listening to the nurturing voice deep inside us that says, 'This is important to you.' The more self-knowledge we have the more likely it is that we will be able to act in accordance with our truest selves."

- "Some women can be disabled by a hangnail, while others could be hit by a truck and keep smiling. The difference involves attitude and coping capacities."

- "In life, as in writing, it is as important to know what to delete as it is to know what to add. We don't want our lives to be one long to-do list filled with musts and shoulds."

There are far, far more jewels of wisdom in this book that I could share with you, but these teasers should be intriguing enough for anyone who is interested in learning more. And why the title? Pipher says, "I chose the word 'rowing' rather than sailing or floating because, to stay on course, we need to make an effort, choose a positive attitude, maintain a strong sense of direction as we travel toward winter…". Perhaps that quote, along with all the others led to her admitting that the core lesson in the book is that "Everything is workable." That of course is another SMART reminder that while we will always face challenges, everything is workable. And let's never, ever forget that the wolf we feed is the one most alive in our world.

Chapter Twenty

Ten Pointers To Living A Well Life

> *"Man does not simply exist but always decides*
> *what his existence will be, and what he will*
> *become the next moment. By the same token,*
> *every human being has the freedom to change*
> *in an instant." ~Viktor Frankl*

A goal for most people I know is to live a well life. But what does that really mean? If we don't pay attention, stay conscious and strive to be proactive, it's likely that we are creating our life by default rather than by design. In other words, we end up reacting to whatever is happening in the world around us—in our families, our workplace or with our health—and if it's good, we are happy. But if any of those outward circumstances takes a nasty turn, we veer off track and end up in the bushes. Only when we consciously choose to design our life, can we claim the reality of a well life.

Fortunately, there is help. A new book by Briana and Dr. Peter Borten titled, *The Well Life* offers dozens of ideas and practices to help us structure a life filled with balance, happiness and peace. Even those of us who have read hundreds of books on self-empowerment, spirituality and positive living can benefit by many of the suggestions offered in this book. And regardless of how old we are or when we happen to pick up this book, who among us can't use a few pointers to ensure that our design is a creation we hope to experience in the days to come?

What Does A Well Life Look Like?

Of course, in order to create a life by design it is important to define what is meant by a well life. According to the authors, a few of those qualities are:

- An experience of ease in our bodies and all our activities;

- A sense of openness and eagerness about the future;

- Authenticity or integrity in the body, spirit, emotions and mind;

- The ongoing desire to expand, create, learn and grow;

- Healthy and fulfilling relationships;

- Financial stability;

- Frequent experiences of laughter, play and enjoyment;

- Other qualities that fit your personal lifestyle;

Three Elements Of A Well Life

At the core of the book are three elements that are essential for a well life. These elements are woven throughout the book as a foundation necessary to keep all aspects of our lives in balance. These three principles work together to ensure that every area of our lives stays balanced and satisfying.

The first element is a sense of SWEETNESS. As the authors say, "Sweetness not only makes life more satisfying, it also makes you stronger and better—more authentically you." The way I understand it, sweetness is what makes our experiences of everything richer and more rewarding. It is the combination of playing, loving, creating, enjoying, being in nature, dancing, laughing and spending time with friends that are so often what makes our hearts sing and feel glad.

The second element is STRUCTURE. The authors explain this in terms of "life architecture." Without good structure or life architecture, the entire foundation of our lives might be overly unsound, complicated or stressful. As explained by the Bortens, "A good structure is one that's forged consciously, incorporates sweetness and space, and steers you in the direction of your dreams."

The final element is SPACE. The authors define this by

saying, "Space is where we listen—not to our thoughts or the media, but to the stillness within us where truth lives." Without space our sweetness may be inauthentic or unconnected to our real self. By the same token, without space, structure loses its perspective and direction. Space, or what we might call emptiness, pulls us out of the perpetual mental engagement that often dominates our lives.

Pointers For A Well Life

1. Mental, emotional and physical STILLNESS allows us to connect more deeply with ourselves and the world around us. Without that ability, the mental overload or the "Human Data Stream" can overwhelm us. The Bortens explain, many of us "have learned to browse through life—to stay shallow—which makes it harder for us to go deep and hold our focus for an extended period." They wisely recommend, "If you need to watch something, watch your breath."

2. Keeping your agreements and doing what you say you're going to do, "could be the most life-changing habit a person could adopt," say the authors. They go on to explain, "Agreements are structures, and healthy agreements make for a healthy life."

3. Most of us aren't clear about what it is that we truly want. A big reason is we don't trust ourselves. We are

also afraid we will make the wrong choice, or that choosing one path will make the other options unavailable. Not true. We can always change our mind and sometimes we will find even more benefits by letting the path unfold as it goes.

4. Understanding the difference between self-worth and self-esteem provides clarity on the path to a greater confidence to do and create the things we choose. According to the Bortens, "Recognition of your self-worth will make you stronger in yourself; good self-esteem can help you take this value into the world and put it into use."

5. Community is essential—but we only thrive when we make our communities intentional. Unless our communities embrace similar values as us, there will always be friction.

6. When we discover what lights us up, it's just like discovering a superpower. As the authors say, "Even if your goals are quite modest, and even if you never reach them, if you're guided by purpose and use your gifts, life won't feel like a missed opportunity."

7. The famous saying by Joseph Campbell, "Follow your bliss" is often misinterpreted. Instead of a blanket endorsement to do whatever you want whenever you want, he actually felt that if you follow your passion then no matter what challenges you encounter along

the way, you will realize they are just part of the journey. Instead, he later came out with, "I wish I had said, 'Follow your blisters.'"

8. Sometimes it is important to be OKAY with the idea of NOT achieving your goals or intentions. That's because if you try too hard, or are afraid that it will never happen, you might actually be putting up obstacles or pushing your good away. If you can relax into the idea of not realizing your intentions enough to recognize the blocks within you, you might discover what needs to be let go of before you can move on. As the authors say, "The thing is, the fear of being poor isn't what makes someone rich, and the fear of being fat isn't what makes someone thin. Aversion may motivate us, but it doesn't produce healthy, lasting, sustainable change."

9. Not everything that happens to you is a result of your thoughts. Sometimes bad things happen to good people no matter what. However, the Bortens believe, "The quality of the lens you see life through is arguably a more significant determinant of your quality of life than your actual circumstances are."

10. According to the authors, planning is "...the STRUCTURE that enables the integration of SWEETNESS and SPACE in your life, so it is a precious thing." What planning allows us to do is to

make our intentions more real. It generates momentum, asserts our position as creators of our lives and aids in necessary discipline. Of course, one should avoid over-planning, but as a practice good planning is a big benefit to a well life.

Believe it or not but I have just barely scratched the top layer of wisdom and practical ideas I found in this book. While some of the pointers I mention might sound similar to other authors and/or books, I was delighted by the amount of new, interesting and helpful information the authors provide.

Of course, like SMART Living or rightsizing, a Well Life is not something you manage to achieve just once. It is an ongoing process of learning, stretching, growing and discovering each and every day. As the authors put it, in a very SMART way, "It's time to stop treating life like a temperamental slot machine—you're not at the mercy of an unconscious thing that delivers random outcomes, determined by luck." Instead, we each have tremendous influence on the shape of our lives, and always on the sweetness, space and structure of every single day. Remember, we get to make it up!

Final Thoughts

*"You become what you give your attention
to...If you yourself don't choose what
thoughts and images you expose yourself to,
someone else will, and their motives may
not be the highest." ~Epictetus*

As I mentioned in the beginning of this book, Thom first came up with the quote, "Every day you can choose to be happy, loving and live life to its fullest...remember you get to make it up." As I've said before, it took even me a while to appreciate the value of what sounds like a fairly simplistic way to look at the world. But I'm now convinced that simple statement is far more transformative than it seems on the surface. Through the years it has become words I live by. While I don't always manage to do it very well, every day I'm getting better as time goes by. And yes, my world is happier and more meaningful because it.

I recently asked Thom what comes up for him when he hears that statement, what he meant all those years ago and still today. He said it is really about choice. The choice to consciously remember that even when we can't control events or circumstances—within ourselves or the world—we each have the choice to be the kind of person we want to be. We also have the choice to live the life we want to live. Yes, we do get to make it up!

I also think it is very wise to remember that if you don't remember that *you* get to *choose*, then chances are very good that someone else will do it for you. Everyone, including loved ones like our parents, siblings, our children and even our spouses have opinions about what we should be doing and how we should live. Even when they love us and care about us, it's often very easy to assert their own needs and desires over our own. After all, who doesn't like to think they know best? But if we relinquish our own choices to please or suit others, then we are like a rudderless boat subject to the whims of chance or weather.

Perhaps even worse, when we don't realize that we do have those choices and that they belong to us alone, then there are less-loving people who can and often do step in to control us. Anyone in authority, be they governmental, institutional or personal—and yes, that includes even those with religious authority—can manipulate and control us to fit to their needs rather than our own. Even when people mean well, and I sincerely hope they do, it will be tempting for them to want to direct us in ways that suit their own agenda first and foremost.

Maybe that is why I've grown to love this statement of "making it up" and the idea behind it so much. The more I move into my own awareness of my choices, the less I am automatically controlled by anyone else. The more I move into my own personal empowerment, the less likely am I to be taken advantage of or swayed into actions or decisions that aren't right for me. And I believe the more I realize that I get to choose, that I am making it up my way, the less likely am I to try to control or direct others as well. That's because when I accept the freedom to make, choose and create my own life, I allow others the same gift.

If you're anything like me, it might take a while for this idea to sink it. Obviously it has taken me a while since I first heard it. But if you stick with it—if you regularly remind yourself of the ideas I've included in this book, and read the many authors who also write about it—it WILL happen. Just never lose the awareness that you can often chose how to act, where to go and what to do—and at the very least you can *always* choose how to respond. I urge you to accept that your life can reflect your hopes, values and dreams. But first and foremost you have to believe, and then remember, that you get to make it up!

ABOUT THE AUTHOR

Kathy Gottberg has authored hundreds of newsletters, articles, blog posts and six books during the last thirty years. Her insatiable curiosity continually leads her imagination, along with her writing, in all sorts of diverse and interesting directions. That's why she has proudly authored five works of nonfiction and one novel. Her current passion is writing and blogging at SMART Living 365.com where she explores practical ideas and experiences that lead to happiness, peace and well-being for all. Also relevant to those paths are positive aging and retirement.

Kathy and her husband Thom have been partners in life and love for the last 43 years. They, and their dog Kloe, live in La Quinta, CA.

Contact The Author Online

https://kathygottberg.com
https://smartliving365.com

Social Media Contacts:

Twitter: **https://twitter.com/gottgreen**
Facebook: **https://www.facebook.com/SMARTLiving365**
Pinterest: **https://www.pinterest.com/gottgreen**
Goodreads: **https://www.goodreads.com/Kathygottberg**

Made in the USA
Middletown, DE
26 May 2022

66293502R00092